Choose what *you* use

The FPA essential guide to contraception

talking sense about sex

Published by
FPA
50 Featherstone Street
London EC1Y 8QU
Tel: 020 7608 5240
Fax: 0845 123 2349

www.fpa.org.uk

MORAY COUNCIL LIBRARIES & INFO.SERVICES	
20 34 07 07	
Askews & Holts	
613.9432	

The Family Planning Association is a registered charity, number 250187, and a limited liability company registered in England, number 887632.
© FPA 2010

Illustrations Leo Cannatella
Posters and postcards BLAC, the Ethical Agency and Feel
Photos www.johnbirdsall.co.uk, Library photos supplied by models
Printed by Newnorth Print Ltd.
Crown copyright material is reproduced under the terms of the Click-Use Licence.
ISBN: 978-1-905506-76-7

This book can only give you basic information about contraception and sexual health. The information is based on evidence-guided research from the World Health Organization, The Faculty of Sexual and Reproductive Healthcare of the Royal College of Obstetricians and Gynaecologists and The British Association of Sexual Health and HIV and National Institute for Health and Clinical Excellence guidance available at the time this book was printed. Different people may give you different information and advice on certain points. All methods of contraception come with a Patient Information Leaflet which provides detailed information about the method.

Remember – contact your doctor, practice nurse or a contraception or sexual health clinic if you are worried or unsure about anything.

Contents

Acknowledgements

We would like to thank all the people who have contributed their valuable time and knowledge to this book:

- All FPA staff who worked on the book.
- Davina McCall.

Foreword by Davina McCall

The launch of the first contraceptive pill in the 1930s, and the arrival of alternative methods since then, has been a fantastic development for the men and women who want to choose when, or whether they have children. Contraception can help to prevent an unplanned pregnancy, protect against sexually transmitted infections and, as a bonus – if you're not worrying about accidentally getting pregnant or catching something nasty – help you to enjoy sex more.

But using contraception, and trying to choose the right method for you, can also be a bit of a minefield. Your doctor may tell you a particular contraceptive is your best option, a magazine says use another, and your friend swears by the method she has. But what method should *you* use? And come to think about it . . . how many methods are there? Not to mention all those myths floating around. Is it really true that hormonal methods are dangerous? Well wonder no more! Reading this really useful, straight-talking book by FPA will answer your questions.

FPA is a respected sexual health charity that has been around for 80 years – and has been talking about contraception for all of that time. It produces millions of booklets and speaks to tens of thousands of men and women about contraception each year. There is no organisation better placed to provide you with this information.

If you have time, start at the beginning of the book and read the questions you ought to ask yourself before choosing a contraceptive. If you don't have time, dip in and out of the chapters to explore each method separately. Your contraceptive needs will change throughout your lifetime so it's a book you can come back to time and time again, perhaps, for example, after you've had a baby.

The book is a great read and I'll certainly keep it on my shelf. It put my mind at rest by quieting those niggling queries I had about contraception and helped me to be proactive about choosing a method for *me*. I hope it does the same for you.

Davina McCall, TV presenter

Useful words

Anaesthetic – A drug that blocks or lessens sensation, affecting the whole body (general anaesthetic) or a part of the body (local anaesthetic).

Bacteria – Simple organisms that are responsible for infections such as the sexually transmitted infections chlamydia, gonorrhoea and syphilis.

Breakthrough bleeding – Bleeding from the vagina that occasionally happens when you are using hormonal contraception.

Circumcision – Surgical procedure to remove the foreskin from the penis.

Cervix – The lower part of the uterus that connects to the vagina.

Clitoris – Sensitive tissue found towards the front of the vulva which, when stimulated, can make women feel sexually aroused and can lead to orgasm.

Conception – The process of getting pregnant that begins with the fertilisation of an egg by a sperm and ends with the implantation of a fertilised egg in the endometrium.

Ectopic pregnancy – A pregnancy that occurs outside the uterus, usually in a fallopian tube. Although it is not common, it is very serious.

Embryo – The products of conception up to the eighth week of pregnancy.

Endometrium – The lining of the uterus. This is shed as a period once a month.

Estrogen – A female sex hormone that is responsible for changes that occur in the menstrual cycle. It also controls female characteristics such as breast growth and the distribution of fat on the thighs and hips.

Fallopian tubes – The small tubes linking the ovaries to the uterus.

Fetus – The unborn child from the eighth week of development.

General practice – Your local healthcare clinic. It is sometimes called the surgery.

General practitioner (GP) – A doctor working in the community who provides health services to a local area.

Hormone – A chemical released in the blood which acts on specific organs in the body.

Hormonal contraception – Methods of contraception that contain the hormones estrogen and progestogen or progestogen alone – similar to the natural hormones women produce in their ovaries.

Hypertension – High blood pressure.

Jaundice – Yellow discolouration of the skin or eyes.

Labia – The inner and outer vaginal lips.

Long-acting reversible contraception – Methods of contraception that do not depend on you remembering to take or use them. They are the IUS, the IUD, the contraceptive injection and the contraceptive implant.

Lubricant – A gel or liquid used on the genitals to help make sex safer, easier, more fun or less painful.

Menopause – The time in a woman's life when the ovaries stop producing eggs, her periods stop and she is no longer fertile. This usually happens when she is around 50 years old.

Menstrual cycle – The process during which an egg develops and is released from the ovaries, and the endometrium prepares for a possible pregnancy.

Menstruation – The monthly loss of the endometrium, also known as a period.

Non-spermicidally lubricated condoms – Condoms with a lubricant that doesn't kill sperm. These are recommended instead of spermicidally lubricated condoms.

Osteoporosis – Loss of bony tissue, resulting in bones that are brittle and more likely to fracture.

Ovaries – Organs on either side of the uterus that produce ova (eggs) in structures called follicles. They also produce the hormones estrogen and progesterone.

Ovulation – The release of an egg from the ovaries each month.

Penis – The male reproductive organ outside the body.

Period – See menstruation.

Premenstrual symptoms – The symptoms that some women experience just before their period is due, and for some time after it starts.

Progesterone – A female sex hormone that is responsible for changes that occur in the menstrual cycle. It also helps to maintain a normal pregnancy.

Protozoan – An organism capable of causing a sexually transmitted infection such as trichomonas.

Scrotum – The soft pouch of skin that holds and protects the testicles.

Semen – The creamy ejaculation fluid that contains sperm.

Sexually transmitted infection also known as STI – An infection that can be caught or passed on by sexual contact.

Sperm – The male sex cell made in the testicles, which joins with the female egg to form an embryo.

Spermicidally lubricated condoms – Condoms that contain a lubricant and a spermicide. If you can, avoid using spermicidally lubricated condoms. The spermicide commonly contains a chemical called Nonoxinol 9, which does not protect against HIV and may even increase the risk of infection.

Spermicide – Chemicals that kill sperm.

Spotting – A small amount of bleeding from the vagina.

Choose what you use, The FPA essential guide to contraception

Testicle – Men have two testicles and they produce sperm and male hormones.

Testosterone – A male hormone that is responsible for sperm production and growth. It is also important for male sex drive and controls the male characteristics such as hair growth and deepening of the voice.

Thrombosis – A blood clot. If the clot occurs in a vein it is a venous thrombosis, or deep vein thrombosis (DVT), and if it occurs in an artery it is an arterial thrombosis.

Toxic shock syndrome – A state of acute shock due to blood poisoning, which can be caused by using tampons. It is a serious illness and the symptoms include a sudden, high fever, being sick, diarrhoea, sore throat and a rash.

Unprotected/unsafe sex – Having sex when you are not protected against sexually transmitted infections or pregnancy.

Urinate – To pass urine through the urethra.

Urethra – Tube through which urine is passed in men and women.

Uterus – Also called the womb. This is where an embryo/fetus develops when a woman becomes pregnant.

Vagina – A muscular tube 7–10cm long that connects the cervix to the vulva.

Vas deferens – The tube that carries sperm from the testicles to the penis.

Virus – A microscopic agent that can cause an infection. Some viruses cause sexually transmitted infections such as genital warts, herpes and HIV.

Vulva – The female genitals outside the body. It includes the entrance to the vagina and urethra, the labia and clitoris.

Withdrawal bleed – A bleed from the vagina which occurs when a woman has a week free from hormonal contraception.

About this book

Do you need to use contraception? Are you wondering which method would be most suitable for you? Did you know there are 15 methods of contraception currently available in the UK?

While choice is a wonderful thing, having 15 methods of contraception to choose from can be overwhelming. Therefore, it's not surprising that many women and their partners let a health professional decide what they should use, or rely on a couple of methods they've used before. The majority of women (aged under 50) in Great Britain use just two methods of contraception – the contraceptive pill and the male condom.[1]

Often this means that lifestyle factors – for example, the type of relationship you are in, your medical history or daily routine – are not taken into account when choosing what contraception to use. As a result, many people don't use the method which is most suitable for them.

Finding contraception that suits you and your lifestyle is essential because:
- it stops you or a partner from becoming pregnant
- you are more likely to use it effectively
- it makes you worry less and therefore is good for general confidence, sexual pleasure and peace of mind.

fpa gratefully acknowledges funding from Bayer Schering Pharma.

Choose your contraception the same way you choose handbags.

Go shopping.

When FPA conducted a survey to explore women's attitudes to choosing contraception we found that more than a quarter of women (aged 18–49 years old) spend less than 15 minutes researching and selecting a method of contraception, and that 15 per cent of women do not spend any time researching and selecting their contraception.

We also found that almost half of all women have had a pregnancy scare – thinking they were, or could be, pregnant when they didn't want to be – and 28 per cent of these women said the reason for that scare was a problem with their contraception, for example, they forgot to take a pill or the condom came off.[2]

There is still a lot to be done to give people the information they need to choose the right contraceptive method. This book was written to provide that information. It explains everything you need to know about *all* of the contraceptive methods available in the UK, answers your concerns, highlights lifestyle and personal factors that you should consider and provides enough details for you to make a full and informed choice.

In this book you will find:
- in-depth information on 15 contraceptive methods and emergency contraception
- an explanation of reproduction and conception
- points to consider about you and your lifestyle before you make any decisions
- a guide to contraception after you've had a baby
- information about sexually transmitted infections
- advice on how to have safer sex
- the options you might want to consider if you are facing an unplanned pregnancy
- useful resources and organisations to help you find out more.

Your contraceptive needs may change over time, for example, if you have a baby or begin a new relationship, so you can dip into this book as and when you need to.

This book is for anyone who wants to protect themselves against pregnancy and sexually transmitted infections. Although it has been written primarily for women, all the information in the book will be useful for men. However, men might be particularly interested in Chapter 13: Male condoms and Chapter 8: Male sterilisation.

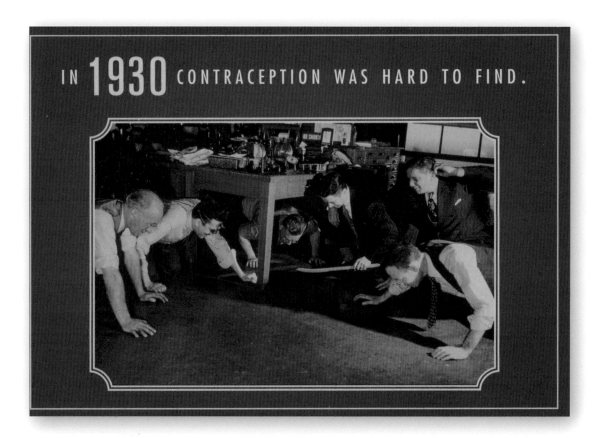

IN **1930** CONTRACEPTION WAS HARD TO FIND.

FPA has been providing sexual health information and advice for over 75 years. The organisation began in the 1930s as the National Birth Control Council and over the course of eight decades has championed free contraception for all, established a network of sexual health clinics (which are now run by the NHS) and campaigned for women to have safe and equal access to abortion. Therefore, we are ideally placed to help you to choose what contraception you use.

Chapter 1: You and your body

Before talking about or choosing contraception it is useful if you know about the male and female reproductive systems, the menstrual cycle and what's involved in conception. With this knowledge it is easier to understand how each contraceptive method prevents a pregnancy, and to decide which method to use.

Women's bodies

The reproductive system in women is made up of external and internal organs. These are found in the lower abdomen, the part of the body below the tummy/belly button. This area is often referred to as the pelvic area.

The external organs, known collectively as the vulva, are the:
- vaginal entrance
- urethral opening
- labia
- clitoris.

The internal organs are the:
- ovaries
- fallopian tubes
- uterus
- cervix
- vagina.

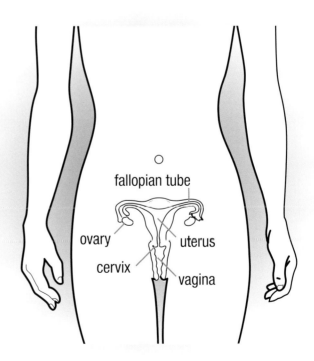

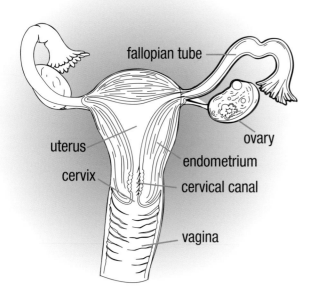

fallopian tube

ovary

uterus

endometrium

cervix

cervical canal

vagina

Ovaries

Women have two ovaries – one on each side of the uterus. They are the size and shape of almonds and they contain ova (eggs) in structures called follicles. The ovaries produce the two female sex hormones – estrogen and progesterone. A hormone is a chemical messenger which is released in the blood to target specific organs. Sex hormones are responsible for sexual development and reproduction.

Fallopian tubes

The two fallopian tubes are found on each side of the uterus, near the ovaries. The funnel-like end of the fallopian tube picks up the egg released by the ovary and helps move the egg along towards the uterus. The inside of the tube is very delicate and can easily be damaged or blocked by infection.

Uterus

The uterus is roughly the size and shape of an upside-down pear. It is hollow, very stretchy and made of muscle. This is where the baby develops if a woman becomes pregnant. The uterus can stretch to hold a baby and shrink more or less back to its pre-pregnancy size after the baby is born.

Cervix

The lower part of the uterus that connects to the vagina is called the cervix. Sperm, released by the man during sex, swim from the vagina through the cervix to reach an egg.

The cervix contains small glands which produce secretions called mucus. Mucus alters in texture and quantity during a woman's menstrual cycle. Around the time of ovulation – when she is in her fertile time – it changes from being thick, sticky and creamy in colour to being clearer, wetter and more stretchy – like raw egg white. These changes allow sperm to pass through the cervix and reach the egg more easily. When a woman is pregnant, the cervix becomes plugged with very thick mucus to protect the developing baby from infection.

Vagina

The vagina is a muscular tube 7–10cm long that leads from the cervix to the vaginal opening. The vaginal opening is between the legs, between the urethra at the front, and the anus at the back. The vagina tilts upward and towards the small of the back. It has glands that produce lubricating secretions when a woman is sexually aroused, which help the penis enter the vagina. Like the uterus, the vaginal walls are stretchy, allowing it to hold a tampon and stretch around a penis during sex or a baby during delivery.

Fast facts

- The fallopian tubes are only as wide as a human hair and roughly 10cm long.
- When a woman reaches puberty she will have up to one million eggs in her ovaries but only about 400–500 will be released at ovulation in her reproductive life.
- An egg is less than 1/8 of the size of a grain of sand and invisible to the naked eye.

The menstrual cycle

The menstrual cycle is the process during which an egg develops and is released from the ovaries, and the endometrium prepares for a possible pregnancy. If a woman does not become pregnant the endometrium is shed as her period. It is controlled by hormones.

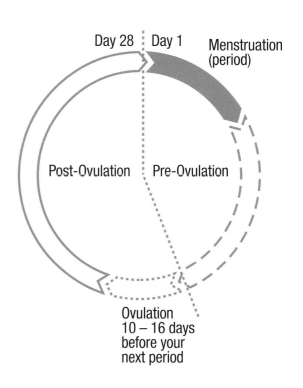

The number of days in the menstrual cycle is calculated from the first day of the period to the day before the start of the next period. The average length of the menstrual cycle is around 28 days, although many women have longer or shorter cycles and this is normal.

A step-by-step guide to the menstrual cycle

- The first day of the period is known as day one of the cycle. When a woman has her period about 20 eggs start to develop in an ovary.
- The hormone estrogen causes the endometrium to start to thicken in preparation for a fertilised egg. It also causes the mucus in the cervix to become thinner, wetter and more stretchy, allowing sperm to reach an egg more easily.
- Regardless of how long or short a woman's cycle is, ovulation will usually happen around 10–16 days before the start of her next period. However, the time from the first day of the period to ovulation can vary between women.
- Occasionally, more than one egg is released during ovulation (this will happen within 24 hours of the first egg being released). If more than one egg is fertilised it can lead to a multiple pregnancy such as twins.
- Ovulation triggers the production of a second hormone, progesterone. This prepares the endometrium even further, ensuring that it is spongy, thick and full of nutrients so that a fertilised egg can implant into it.
- After ovulation the cervical mucus goes back to being thick and sticky. If the egg is not fertilised it is reabsorbed naturally by the body, the level of hormones falls, and this menstrual cycle comes to an end.
- The cycle then begins again. The endometrium breaks down and is shed through the vagina as a period, also called menstruation.

Fast facts

- The average amount of blood lost during a period is 3–5 tablespoons.
- Women living together often find that they have their periods at the same time.
- Some menstrual cycles can be as short as 21 days and some as long as 40 days.

Menopause

When a woman is around 50 years old, her ovaries stop producing eggs, her periods stop and she is no longer fertile. This is called the menopause.

The time leading up to the menopause is called the perimenopause, and it is during this time that the hormonal and biological changes associated with the menopause begin. For example, a woman's periods could become more or less frequent, or shorter, before stopping altogether. Her contraceptive needs change during this time. She will be unable to use some methods of contraception and eventually will not need to use any because it is no longer possible for her to get pregnant. Health professionals usually advise that you should use contraception until you have not had a period or any bleeding for two years if you are under 50, or one year if you are over 50.

Men's bodies

Unlike women's reproductive organs, men's are found entirely outside the body.

Penis

The penis is the external male reproductive organ. Urine and semen come out of it. It has two main parts, the head and the shaft. The head is surrounded by a sleeve of skin called the foreskin. Some men have their foreskin removed by surgery, this is called circumcision.

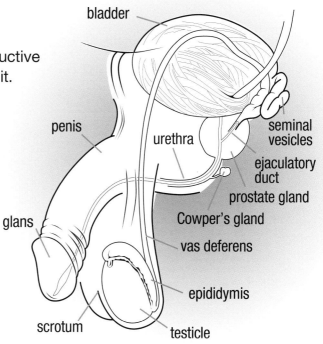

Usually the penis is soft and hangs down over the scrotum but it can become erect. When a man is sexually excited (and at other times too) the penis fills with blood and becomes stiff, grows longer and wider and sticks outwards and upwards from his body. The foreskin also stretches to leave the head of the penis completely exposed.

The shape of an erect penis varies although it usually curves upwards slightly, and may point to one side. Penis size also varies but not by very much. Adult penis size is usually between 8.5cm–10.5cm (3–4 inches) long when soft, and between 15cm–18cm (6–7 inches) when hard.

Testicles and scrotum

The testicles are the male equivalent of a woman's ovaries. Inside the testicles sperm are made and important male hormones are produced. Men have two testicles, roughly the size of two small plums, and they are protected in a soft pouch of skin called the scrotum.

The scrotum hangs outside the body just behind the penis and between the legs. Its position helps the testicles to keep cool – the average body temperature (37°C) is too hot to produce healthy sperm. Testicles are very sensitive to heat – if they get too hot the scrotum drops down to cool off and if they get too cold the scrotum shrinks closer to the body to keep warm.

Male hormones

Hormones are just as important for reproduction in men as they are in women. The testicles produce the male hormone testosterone, which is responsible for sperm production and growth. It is also important for male sex drive and controls the male characteristics such as hair growth and the deepening of the voice.

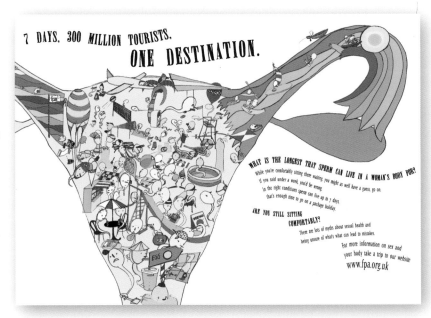

7 DAYS, 300 MILLION TOURISTS, ONE DESTINATION.

WHAT IS THE LONGEST THAT SPERM CAN LIVE IN A WOMAN'S BODY FOR?
While you're comfortably sitting there waiting you might as well have a guess, go on.
If you said under a week, you'd be wrong.
In the right conditions sperm can live up to 7 days,
that's enough time to go on a package holiday.

ARE YOU STILL SITTING COMFORTABLY?
There are lots of myths about sexual health and being unsure of what's what can lead to mistakes.

For more information on sex and your body take a trip to our website
www.fpa.org.uk

Sperm

Inside each testicle there are about 1,000 tightly coiled tubes. Individual sperm are continuously made in these tubes. The growing sperm travel along the tiny tubes to a larger coiled tube called the epididymis, which is at the top of the testicle. They stay here until they are fully mature and ready to be ejaculated.

Ejaculation

At ejaculation sperm passes along the vas deferens to the penis and out of the body through the urethra. On the way, fluid from the seminal vesicles and prostate gland is added to the sperm. This helps to nourish and transport them and gives semen (as it is now called) its white, creamy appearance.

Fast facts

- The average ejaculation contains up to 300 million sperm and will fill a teaspoon.
- Sperm are tiny – only 1/25mm long – about one hundred times smaller than the female egg.
- On average men produce around 150–1,000 million sperm everyday, so they are unlikely to run out.

Conception

Conception is a process that begins with fertilisation and ends with implantation – getting pregnant. For fertilisation to take place an egg needs to meet a sperm – usually through a man and a woman having sex.

A step-by-step guide to conception

The ovary releases an egg as part of the menstrual cycle and it is picked up by the fallopian tube. Here it can be fertilised by sperm. Sperm are able to wait around in the uterus and fallopian tube until ovulation, although only a small number of sperm will actually survive the trip to the fallopian tubes.

about 1½ days later: the fertilised egg splits into two cells

about 3–4 days later: the fertilised egg is now 64 separate cells

about two days later: the cells divide again

5–6 days later: the embryo floats in the uterus

fallopian tube

uterus

ovary

the embryo starts to embed itself in the uterus wall. This is around 10 days after ovulation and pregnancy begins

cervix

START HERE

vagina

ovulation occurs; an egg is released from the ovary into the fallopian tube. It lives for up to 24 hours, if unprotected sex has taken place sperm surround the egg. One breaks through to fertilise it.

Small beating hairs and tiny wave-like contractions help the egg travel along the fallopian tube where it may meet a sperm within minutes or hours of ovulation. The egg only lives for up to 24 hours so the chance of pregnancy is increased if the sperm is ready and waiting. If you have sex 2–3 times a week you will ensure there is always sperm waiting.

The sperm attaches itself to the egg and produces a special substance that dissolves the outer coat of the egg. Only one sperm will be able to enter the egg and once it has entered, the egg coating is repaired to prevent other sperm from getting in. Once the sperm is fully inside the egg, fertilisation has taken place.

The fertilised egg is wafted down the fallopian tube to the ready-prepared uterus. Here, the embryo settles and over a few days attaches itself to the thick, nutritious lining. Implantation has now taken place, conception is complete and pregnancy begins. The time from ovulation to implantation is about 10 days.

Once the pregnancy has begun, the pregnancy hormone, human chorionic gonadotrophin (hCG) is produced. This is what is looked for and detected in pregnancy tests.

Fast facts

- Sperm can swim through the cervix and into the uterus to meet an egg in about two minutes.
- The egg can be fertilised by sperm that have been ejaculated up to seven days before.
- It takes about three hours for a sperm to fully enter the egg.

Useful organisations

- FPA
- your general practice
- a contraception or sexual health clinic
- a young person's service
- a genitourinary medicine (GUM) clinic
- Brook
- Health and Social Care in Northern Ireland
- Health of Wales Information service
- NHS Direct
- NHS Scotland

Contact details are listed in Chapter 22: Useful organisations.

Chapter 2: Your lifestyle, your choice – an introduction to contraception

What is contraception?

Contraception is the use of hormones (for example, the combined pill), a device (for example, the IUD) or procedure (for example, sterilisation) to help stop a woman getting pregnant. Some contraceptive methods may also help to protect against sexually transmitted infections. Contraception is sometimes known as birth control or family planning.

Using contraception is the only way to help protect yourself from an unplanned pregnancy. A woman (who is not using contraception) **can** still get pregnant if:

- it's the first time she has had sex
- she doesn't have an orgasm
- a man pulls out of her vagina before he comes
- she has sex when she has her period
- she has sex standing up
- she uses a douche to rinse out her vagina. This can be harmful.

Choosing a contraceptive method is about finding one that fits in with you and your lifestyle. It should not just stop you or a partner from becoming pregnant but should give you general confidence and peace of mind. Using the correct contraception for you can also increase your sexual pleasure because you are not worrying about becoming pregnant and – if you are using condoms – getting a sexually transmitted infection. Therefore you can relax and enjoy yourself more!

The good news is that there are 15 methods to choose from! These are:
1. Contraceptive injections
2. Contraceptive implant
3. Intrauterine system (IUS)
4. Intrauterine device (IUD)
5. Female sterilisation

6. Male sterilisation
7. Contraceptive patch
8. Contraceptive vaginal ring
9. Combined pill
10. Progestogen-only pill
11. Male condom
12. Female condom
13. Diaphragms
14. Cap
15. Natural family planning

You may also need to use emergency contraception – the emergency contraceptive pill and the emergency IUD.

So how does contraception work?

Contraception works in different ways but generally prevents pregnancy by preventing the sperm and egg from meeting or by interrupting the menstrual cycle, the activity of the male or female reproductive organs or the process of conception.

Some contraceptives contain hormones. These are the combined pill, the progestogen-only pill, the intrauterine system, the contraceptive implant, the contraceptive injection, the contraceptive vaginal ring and the contraceptive patch, and emergency hormonal contraception. They work by releasing the hormones estrogen and progestogen together, or progestogen alone. This can:
- stop ovulation
- thicken the cervical mucus to prevent sperm from reaching an egg
- thin the endometrium to prevent a fertilised egg implanting.

The IUD does not release hormones, but it stops the sperm reaching an egg and may also prevent a fertilised egg from implanting in the uterus.

Barrier methods, such as the male and female condom, diaphragm and cap are used inside or outside of the body to prevent sperm from reaching an egg.

In male sterilisation the vas deferens is cut, sealed or blocked to prevent sperm from being ejaculated and therefore meeting an egg. In female sterilisation the fallopian tubes are cut, sealed or blocked to prevent the egg from meeting sperm.

Natural family planning allows a woman to closely monitor the fertile and infertile times of her menstrual cycle so that she can have sex when there is no risk of pregnancy.

For more detailed information on each of these methods, see Chapters 3–18.

Decisions, decisions

The first thing to think about is what type of contraception might suit you best. For example, you may have a preference for hormonal or non-hormonal methods, barrier methods or a method which identifies your fertility cycle.

There are also methods that do not depend on you remembering to take or use them – **no user failure methods**. These methods are often known as long-acting reversible contraceptives – or LARCs. With other methods you have to use or think about them regularly or each time you have sex. You **must** use them according to instructions. These are known as **user failure methods**.

Hormonal methods – *contain estrogen and progestogen or progestogen alone*
The injection, implant, IUS, patch, vaginal ring, combined pill and progestogen-only pill.

Non-hormonal methods – *do not contain any hormones*
The IUD, male and female sterilisation, male and female condoms, the diaphragm or cap and natural family planning.

Barrier methods – *prevent the sperm from meeting an egg*
Male and female condoms and the diaphragm or cap.

Methods with no user failure or LARCs
The IUS, IUD, injection and implant.

Methods with user failure
The patch, vaginal ring, combined pill, progestogen-only pill, male and female condoms, the diaphragm or cap and natural family planning.

Permanent methods
Male and female sterilisation.

Emergency methods
The emergency contraceptive pill and the emergency IUD.

Lifestyle and personal factors
Don't worry if this already seems like a lot of decisions to make – a health professional will be able to help you to find a method that is suitable. However, your best choice is a method that also suits *you* and *your* lifestyle. Asking yourself the following questions may help you think about what you want before you see your health professional, therefore allowing you to make the best personal decisions alongside professional guidance.

When do you want to become pregnant – now, in the near future, many years away, or not at all?
Perhaps you and your partner are thinking about having a baby soon. If you want to have a baby in the next year, pick a contraceptive method that is easily reversible. When you stop using most methods your fertility returns quickly. It can take longer to return if you use the contraceptive injection.

Are you having sex with a new partner?
If you are worried about getting a sexually transmitted infection you should always use condoms, even if you are using another contraceptive method as well.

Are you very certain that you do not want children or do not want any more children?
If you are absolutely certain that you don't want children, or you don't want any more children, you (or a partner) may want to think about sterilisation. This is a permanent method for people who are sure they never want children or do not want more children.

Do you have religious or other views that may affect the type of contraception that you use?
Your religious beliefs or personal values may prevent you from using some methods of contraception. Natural family planning allows you to monitor your fertility using body temperature and cervical secretions. Therefore, this may be suitable for you.

Does your partner have views about what kind of method you should use?

Your partner may have opinions or suggestions about what method of contraception you could use and you can talk to them about their ideas. However, remember that it is important that you use the right method for you based on your own judgment, not the judgment of somebody else.

Do you want to avoid having a period or withdrawal bleed?

If you want to miss out a bleed, for example if you are going on holiday, you can use the combined pill, the patch and the vaginal ring continuously. If you don't have the pill-, patch-, or ring-free week then you will not bleed.

Do you want periods that are lighter, shorter or less painful?

Perhaps your periods are heavy, long and painful. Using the IUS, the patch, the combined pill, or the vaginal ring may make them lighter, shorter or less painful – and therefore easier to manage.

Would you like to control your withdrawal bleed?

Do you like to know exactly when you are due to have your withdrawal bleed so that you can plan around it? The patch, vaginal ring or combined pill might be suitable for you.

If you can't face thinking about contraception every night, there is a better alternative.

Do you prefer not having to think about contraception?

If you are forgetful or your busy day doesn't give you time to think about using contraception regularly the IUD, IUS, implant and injection might be suitable. Once you start using them you don't have to think about them every day or before sex.

Do you want to take a pill every day?

If you don't like stopping and starting pills and would like to take one every day, progestogen-only pills or a combined EveryDay pill might be suitable.

Is it difficult for you to take a pill at the same time every day?

Perhaps you work shifts and can't guarantee that you'll be awake at the same time each day. The progestogen-only pill may not be suitable for you as there is only a small window of time you can take it in. One of the long-acting reversible contraceptives such as the IUD, IUS, injection or implant may be a better option.

Are you interested to know how your fertility cycle works?

Natural family planning teaches you to identify the signs of fertility in your cycle so that you can plan or avoid a pregnancy.

If you can't face thinking about contraception every night, there is a better alternative than this.

How do you feel about trying a new method?

Perhaps you haven't been able to find a method that suits you yet. Try something new!

Are you approaching the menopause?

Women around the age of 50, or those approaching the menopause, may not be able to use the combined pill, the vaginal ring or the patch and may have to switch to another method at this time. A health professional will be able to advise you about your options.

Have you been pregnant recently?

If you have recently been pregnant (had a baby, miscarriage or abortion) a health professional will be able to help you choose a method that is suitable for you and will advise you on when you should start using it.

Do you smoke?

If you smoke some methods may not be suitable for you. Ask a health professional for advice.

Are you overweight?

If you are very overweight certain methods may not be suitable for you. A health professional will be able to advise you.

Are you sensitive to latex or copper?

If you are sensitive to latex (rubber) you should avoid latex condoms and latex diaphragms and caps. Polyurethane (plastic) male and female condoms and silicone diaphragms and caps are available as an alternative. If you are sensitive to copper you will not be able to use the IUD, which is made from plastic and copper.

Do you have any health conditions that might affect your choice?

Women with certain health conditions won't be able to use some methods. Seek advice from your doctor or nurse.

Has a member of your family suffered from any serious medical conditions in the past?

If you have certain conditions in your immediate family's medical history, for example if a family member had a heart attack, venous thrombosis or stroke before they were 45 years old, you may not be able to use certain methods. Tell your doctor or nurse about any conditions you think might be relevant and they will advise you.

Do you get premenstrual symptoms?

Some women experience premenstrual symptoms just before their period is due, and for some time after it starts. If you find these hard to manage you may benefit from taking the combined pill, which can help relieve premenstrual symptoms in some women.

Is it possible that you have a sexually transmitted infection?

If you have a sexually transmitted infection or think it's possible that you might, it is important that you have a check-up and get treatment. To avoid passing the infection on, you should use male or female condoms, either as your main method of contraception, or use them with your regular method.

Are you a man that wants to be in control of your own contraception rather than rely on a partner?

Perhaps *you* want to make sure that a partner doesn't get pregnant. Male condoms are a great choice because they are widely available, don't have any medical side effects and help protect you against sexually transmitted infections too.

Is your partner happy with her method?
A woman may try a lot of different methods of contraception and decide that she doesn't really want to use any of them, or is tired of being responsible for contraception. Find out more about all the different methods using this book. Male condoms and male sterilisation are both methods of contraception for men.

You will find an overview of all the contraceptive methods in the table on page 34. In-depth information about each method is given in Chapters 3–18.

You may know a contraceptive method by its brand name (the name given to it by the manufacturers). There are so many different brand names that we haven't used them in this book, except where it's important to know the brand you are using. Or you may come across or be using a different contraceptive method that is available in another country, which this book doesn't cover. Remember, you can always get advice from a health professional or from any of the organisations listed at the end of this chapter.

Where can I get contraception?

Contraception is **free** for women and men of **all** ages through the National Health Service. You can obtain free contraception, including emergency contraception, from:
- a general practice, unless they say they don't provide contraceptive services
- a contraception clinic or sexual health clinic
- a young person's service (these will have an upper age limit)
- some genitourinary medicine (GUM) clinics.

You can also get free emergency contraception from:
- most NHS walk-in centres (England only) and minor injuries units
- some hospital accident and emergency departments (phone to check first)
- some pharmacies (there may be an age limit).

Contraception is free even if your service gives you a prescription to take to the pharmacy.

Not all services supply all methods – but they should be able to give you information about what contraceptive choices there are and tell you where you can go to get them.

Setting the record straight

As well as the facts there are also countless myths about contraception. The good news is that none of them are true!

Myth busting

Myth: Contraception is a woman's responsibility

Truth: There are two male contraceptive methods. Men can use condoms and men who are sure they don't want any (more) children can be sterilised. More importantly though, men can discuss contraception with their partner and support her in the decision making process.

Myth: Men are not interested in contraception

Truth: An FPA survey revealed that 94 per cent of men aged 18–45 years old in the UK agreed that using contraception is the joint responsibility of men and women and 60 per cent said that men and women should always discuss using contraception together.[3]

Myth: There is no method that protects you from a sexually transmitted infection

Truth: Male and female condoms can help to protect you from sexually transmitted infections.

Myth: All hormonal methods are dangerous

Truth: All methods have disadvantages and risks but if you seek the advice of a health professional and use a method that is suitable for you, hormonal methods are unlikely to harm you. Women have been using hormonal contraception safely for many decades.

Myth: Hormonal methods make you infertile

Truth: If you use a hormonal method your periods and fertility will return to normal soon after you stop using it. The time it takes for this to happen may be different for each woman and for each method but hormonal contraception does not make you infertile.

Buying contraception

If you are aged 16 or over you can buy the emergency contraceptive pill from most pharmacies for around £25. They also sell condoms, diaphragms, caps and spermicide. Condoms are widely available and can be bought from a pharmacy, online or by mail order, as well as from vending machines, supermarkets, garages and other shops.

You can also pay for some methods of contraception (including emergency contraception) at fee-paying clinics. See Chapter 22: Useful organisations.

Contraception for under 16s

Young people under the age of 16 *can* be prescribed contraception and they can get free information and help about contraception from:

- a young person's service
- a contraception clinic or sexual health clinic
- a general practice, unless they say they don't provide contraceptive services
- some GUM clinics.

All services are confidential, which means they won't tell anyone else a young person has used them. However, they may need to involve other services if they believe the young person or someone else, to be at risk of harm (such as physical or sexual abuse). They will discuss this with the young person.

How do I find out about local contraception services?

- You can find out about all sexual health services from **sexual health direct**, run by FPA, on 0845 122 8690 or at **www.fpa.org.uk**.
- You can find details of general practices and pharmacies in England at www.nhs.uk and in Wales at www.wales.nhs.uk. In Scotland you can find details of general practices at www.show.scot.nhs.uk. In England and Wales you can also can also call NHS Direct on 0845 46 47 and in Scotland NHS 24 on 0845 4 24 24 24. In Northern Ireland call The FPA helpline on 0845 122 8687 or for details of general practices see www.n.i.nhs.uk.
- You can also get details of your nearest contraception, GUM or sexual health clinic from a telephone directory, health centre, local pharmacy, hospital,

midwife, health visitor or advice centre.
- For young people's services contact Brook on 0808 802 1234 or Sexwise on 0800 28 29 30.

What to expect from a contraception service

If it's the first time you've used a service you will normally be asked to fill in a form with your name and address.

The health professional may then ask you about your medical and sexual history in order to get an idea of the most suitable contraception for you. For example, if you have hypertension, the combined pill may not be suitable. If you choose certain methods of contraception you may need to have an internal examination, have your blood pressure taken or you may be offered a test for sexually transmitted infections. You will not need to have a routine breast examination or a cervical screening test.

All services, including general practices, are confidential. This means that your personal information, any information about your visit and the tests, treatments or contraception that you've been given will not be shared outside that service without your permission. Don't be afraid to ask if you are not sure who will see your information.

However, health professionals may need to involve other services if they believe you, or another person, to be at significant risk of harm (such as physical or sexual abuse). They will discuss this with you.

Contraception services sometimes provide more than contraception so ask about:
- pre-pregnancy advice/pregnancy testing
- help and advice on an unplanned pregnancy (including keeping the baby, abortion and adoption)
- safer sex advice
- advice on sexual problems
- cervical screening tests and breast awareness
- checks for sexually transmitted infections
- menopause advice
- infertility advice.

Everyone has a right to access health services. If you have special requirements (such as a disability, or if English is not your first language) contact the general practice or clinic in advance to make sure it can meet your needs. In some circumstances you may be able to be seen at home.

Useful organisations

- FPA
- your general practice
- a contraception or sexual health clinic
- a young person's service
- a GUM clinic
- bpas
- Brook
- Marie Stopes
- Health and Social Care in Northern Ireland
- Health of Wales Information Service
- NHS Direct
- NHS Scotland
- Sexwise

Contact details are listed in Chapter 22: Useful organisations.

Effectiveness: How effective any contraceptive is depends on how old you are, how often you have sex and whether you follow the instructions. If 100 sexually active women don't use any contraception, 80 to 90 will become pregnant in a year.

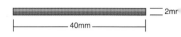

	Contraceptive injection	Implant
What is it?	• An injection of progestogen.	• A small, flexible rod put under the skin of the upper arm releases progestogen.
Effectiveness	• Over 99%.	• Over 99%.
Advantage	• Lasts for eight or 12 weeks – you don't have to think about contraception during this time.	• Works for three years but can be taken out sooner.
Disadvantage	• Can't be removed from the body so side effects may continue while it works and for some time afterwards.	• It requires a small procedure to fit and remove it.

Methods with user failure – you have to use

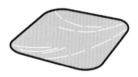

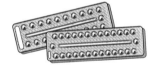

	Contraceptive patch	Contraceptive vaginal ring	Combined pill (COC)	Progestogen (POP)
What is it?	• A small patch stuck to the skin releases estrogen and progestogen.	• A small, flexible, plastic ring put into the vagina releases estrogen and progestogen.	• A pill containing estrogen and progestogen, taken orally.	• A pill contai progestogen,
	Effective only if used according to instructions ... Effective only if			
Effectiveness	• Over 99%.	• Over 99%.	• Over 99%.	• Over 99%.
Advantage	• Can make bleeds regular, lighter and less painful.	• One ring stays in for three weeks – you don't have to think about contraception every day.	• Often reduces bleeding, period pain and premenstrual symptoms.	• Can be used who smoke ar 35, or those w breastfeeding.
Disadvantage	• May be seen and can cause skin irritation.	• You must be comfortable with inserting and removing it.	• Missing pills, vomiting or severe diarrhoea can make it less effective.	• Late pills, vo severe diarrho it less effectiv

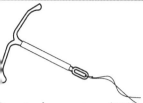

trauterine system (IUS)

- A small, T-shaped, ogestogen-releasing, plastic device out into the uterus.

- Over 99%.

- Works for five years but can be taken t sooner. Periods usually become nter, shorter and less painful.

- rregular bleeding or spotting is mmon in the first six months.

Intrauterine device (IUD)

- A small plastic and copper device is put into the uterus.

- Over 99%.

- Can stay in 5–10 years depending on type but can be taken out sooner.

- Periods may be heavier, longer or more painful.

Female and male sterilisation

- The fallopian tubes in women or the tubes carrying sperm in men (vas deferens) are cut, sealed or blocked.

- The failure rate of female sterilisation is one in 200, and one in 2,000 for male sterilisation.

- Sterilisation is permanent with no long or short-term serious side effects.

- Should not be chosen if in any doubt about having children in the future.

think about them regularly or each time you have sex

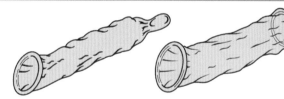

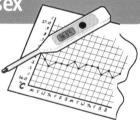

Male condom

- A very thin latex (rubber) or polyurethane (plastic) sheath that is put over the erect penis.

Female condom

- Soft, thin polyurethane sheath that loosely lines the vagina and covers the area just outside.

Diaphragm/cap with spermicide

- A flexible latex (rubber) or silicone device, used with spermicide, is put into the vagina to cover the cervix.

Natural family planning

- Fertile and infertile times of the menstrual cycle are identified by noting different fertility indicators.

cording to instructions ... Effective only if used according to instructions ...

- 98%.

- 95%.

- 92–96%.

- If used according to teaching, up to 99% effective.

Condoms are the best way to help protect yourself against sexually transmitted infections.

- Can be put in any time before sex.

- No chemicals or physical products means no physical side effects.

- May slip off or split if not used correctly or if wrong size or shape.

- Not as widely available as male condoms.

- Putting it in can interrupt sex. If you have sex again extra spermicide is needed.

- Need to avoid sex or use a condom at fertile times of the cycle.

Chapter 3: Contraceptive injections

Contraceptive injections contain a progestogen hormone which is similar to the natural progesterone that women produce in their ovaries. There are two types of injection – Depo-Provera protects you from pregnancy for 12 weeks and Noristerat protects you for eight weeks. Both of these are very effective hormonal methods of contraception.

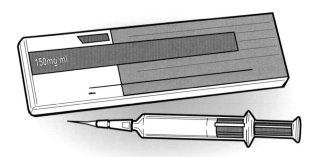

Myth busting

- **Myth: A contraceptive injection causes depression**
  Truth: Mood changes can occur when you are using a contraceptive injection but it doesn't cause depression.

- **Myth: A contraceptive injection is only used by people with learning disabilities**
  Truth: Most women can use the contraceptive injection, not just women with learning disabilities. Check with your doctor or nurse to make sure it is suitable for you.

- **Myth: A contraceptive injection is a last resort method**
  Truth: Lots of women use a contraceptive injection as their first choice method.

How effective is a contraceptive injection?
Contraceptive injections are over 99 per cent effective. This means that less than four women in every 1,000 will get pregnant over two years. Depo-Provera is more effective than Noristerat. The injection is a long-acting reversible contraceptive. *All* long-acting methods are very effective because while they are being used you do not have to remember to take or use contraception.

How do contraceptive injections work?

The main way they work is to stop ovulation each month. They also:

- Thicken the mucus from your cervix. This makes it difficult for sperm to move through it and reach an egg.
- Makes the endometrium thinner so it is less likely to accept a fertilised egg.

Where can I get a contraceptive injection?

Only a doctor or nurse can give you a contraceptive injection. You can go to a contraception or sexual health clinic or to the doctor or nurse at a general practice. All treatment is free and confidential.

How is a contraceptive injection given?

The hormone is injected into a muscle, usually in your bottom. Depo-Provera can also sometimes be given in the arm. Noristerat is a thicker solution so you may find the injection is slightly more painful when it is given. If you want to carry on using this method of contraception, you will need to have injections every 12 weeks if you have Depo-Provera injections, or every eight weeks if you have Noristerat.

You do not need to have a vaginal examination or a cervical screening test to have a contraceptive injection.

Can anyone use a contraceptive injection?

Most women can have a contraceptive injection. Your doctor or nurse will need to ask you about your own and your family's medical history to make sure a contraceptive injection is suitable. Do mention any illness or operations you have had. Some of the conditions which **may** mean you should not use a contraceptive injection are:

- you think you might already be pregnant
- you do not want your periods to change
- you want a baby within the next year.

You have now or have had in the past:

- breast cancer or breast cancer within the last five years
- unexplained vaginal bleeding (for example, bleeding between periods or after sex)
- thrombosis in any vein or artery
- arterial disease or history of serious heart disease or stroke

- diabetes with complications or diabetes for more than 20 years
- active disease of the liver
- risk factors for osteoporosis (see *Can I use a contraceptive injection if I am at risk of osteoporosis?* on page 39).

What are the advantages of the contraceptive injection?
- You don't have to think about contraception for as long as the injection lasts.
- It doesn't interrupt sex.
- You can use it if you are breastfeeding.
- Depo-Provera and Noristerat are not affected by other medicines.
- It may reduce heavy painful periods and help with premenstrual symptoms for some women.
- It may give you some protection against cancer of the uterus.
- It is a good method if you cannot use estrogens, like those in the combined pill.

What are the disadvantages of a contraceptive injection?
- Your periods may change in a way that is not acceptable to you (see *Will a contraceptive injection affect my periods?* on page 40.
- Irregular bleeding may continue for some months after you stop the injections.
- Women may put on weight when they use Depo-Provera (see *Will my weight be affected by a contraceptive injection?* on page 40).
- The injection works for 12 or eight weeks, depending on which type you have. It cannot be removed from your body, so if you have any side effects, you have to be prepared for them to continue during this time and for some time afterwards.
- Your periods, and fertility, may take a few months to return to normal after stopping Depo-Provera injections. Sometimes this can take up to a year.
- Contraceptive injections do not protect you against sexually transmitted infections, so you may have to use condoms as well.

Are there any risks?

- Using Depo-Provera may affect your bones (see *How does Depo-Provera affect my bones?* below).
- Research about the risk of breast cancer and hormonal contraception is complex and contradictory. Research suggests that women who use hormonal contraception appear to have a small increase in risk of being diagnosed with breast cancer compared to women who don't use hormonal contraception. Further research is ongoing.
- You can have an allergic reaction to the injection, but this is rare.
- As with any injection there is a risk of a small infection at the site of the injection.

Your doctor or nurse should discuss all risks and benefits with you.

How does Depo-Provera affect my bones?

Using Depo-Provera affects your natural estrogen levels, causing thinning of the bones. This is not normally a problem for most women as the bone replaces itself when you stop the injection and it does not appear to cause any long-term problems. It does not cause an increase in bone fracture.

Thinning of the bones may be more of a problem for women who already have risk factors for osteoporosis (see *Can I use a contraceptive injection if I am at risk of osteoporosis?* below).

Women under 18 years old may use Depo-Provera, but only after careful evaluation by a doctor or nurse. This is because young women under 18 are still making bone.

Can I use a contraceptive injection if I am at risk of osteoporosis?

If you have risk factors for osteoporosis it is normally advisable to use another method of contraception. Your doctor or nurse will talk to you about this. These factors include:

- a lack of estrogen due to early menopause (before 45 years)
- a lack of estrogen due to missing periods for six months or more, as a result of over-exercising, extreme dieting or eating disorders
- smoking
- heavy drinking
- long-term use of steroids
- a close family history of osteoporosis
- certain medical conditions affecting the liver, thyroid and digestive system.

You can help to make your bones healthier by doing regular weight-bearing exercise such as running and walking, eating a healthy diet adequate in calcium and vitamin D, and cutting down on drinking alcohol and smoking.

The National Osteoporosis Society can give you more information (see Chapter 22: Useful organisations).

Should I have my bones scanned before I start a contraceptive injection?
It is not recommended that all women have a bone scan before they start a contraceptive injection. It may be useful for some women – usually those who have been identified as having risk factors for osteoporosis.

Will a contraceptive injection affect my periods?
Your periods will probably change.
- In some women periods will stop completely (this does not mean you are pregnant).
- Some women will have irregular periods or spotting, especially to begin with.
- Some women will have periods that last longer and are heavier.

These changes may be a nuisance but they are not harmful. If you do have prolonged bleeding it may be possible for the doctor or nurse to give you some additional hormone or medicine that can help control the bleeding. They may also check that the bleeding is not due to other causes, such as an infection.

Will my weight be affected by a contraceptive injection?
Depo-Provera is associated with an increase in weight of up to 3kg (6.6lbs) over two years.

When can I start using a contraceptive injection?
You can start a contraceptive injection any time in your menstrual cycle if it is certain that you are not pregnant. If you start it during the first five days of your period you will be immediately protected against pregnancy.

If you have it on any other day you will not be protected for the first seven days, so you will need to use additional contraception, such as condoms, during this time.

I've just had a baby. Can I use a contraceptive injection?
A contraceptive injection is usually given from six weeks after you have given

birth. Waiting until then makes it less likely that you will have heavy and irregular bleeding.

If you want to use a contraceptive injection before six weeks it can be started three weeks (21 days) after you have given birth. If you start it before day 21 you will be protected from pregnancy immediately. If it is started later than day 21 you will need to use additional contraception for seven days.

A contraceptive injection can be used safely while you are breastfeeding and will not affect your milk supply.

Can I use a contraceptive injection after a miscarriage or abortion?
A contraceptive injection can be started immediately after an abortion or miscarriage. You will be protected against pregnancy immediately.

Can anything make a contraceptive injection less effective?
While a contraceptive injection is working nothing will make it less effective. Injectable contraception is **not** affected by:
- prescribed medicines, including any kind of antibiotics
- any medicines which you buy over the counter at a pharmacy in the UK
- diarrhoea
- vomiting.

It is important to go back at the right time for your next injection – every 12 weeks for Depo-Provera or every eight weeks for Noristerat. If you miss the next injection it may mean that you are no longer protected against pregnancy. To ensure that you remain protected against pregnancy you should not be more than two weeks late for your next injection.

Will I be able to choose which contraceptive injection I use?
It is most likely that you will be offered the injection Depo-Provera as Noristerat is usually only used for short periods of time, for example while waiting for a sterilisation operation to become effective. Your doctor or nurse can discuss with you which contraceptive injection is most suitable.

What should I do if I think that I am pregnant?
Contraceptive injections are a highly effective method of contraception. If you have had your injections on time, it is very unlikely that you will become pregnant.

If you think that you might be pregnant then do a pregnancy test or speak to your doctor or nurse as soon as possible. Using the contraceptive injection does not affect a pregnancy test. If you do get pregnant while you are using a contraceptive injection, there is no evidence that it will harm the baby.

How long can I use a contraceptive injection for?
You can continue to use Depo-Provera until you are 50 years old, provided there are no medical reasons not to use it and you are not at risk of osteoporosis (see *How does Depo-Provera affect my bones?* on page 39). If you do use a contraceptive injection long-term you should expect to have your risk factors for osteoporosis re-assessed every two years. The doctor or nurse may ask you about your lifestyle and discuss whether it would be more suitable for you to use a different method of contraception.

What should I do if I want to stop using a contraceptive injection or try to get pregnant?
If you want to stop a contraceptive injection all you need to do is not have your next injection. Your periods and natural fertility may take a while to return after you stop using a contraceptive injection. However, it is possible to get pregnant before your first period. If you don't wish to become pregnant then you should use another method of contraception from the day that your injection would have been due. If you have sex without using another method of contraception you may want to consider using emergency contraception (see Chapter 17: Emergency contraception).

If you want to try for a baby start pre-pregnancy care such as taking folic acid, stopping smoking and reducing how much alcohol you drink. You can ask your doctor or nurse for further advice.

If I have to go into hospital for an operation should I stop using a contraceptive injection?
No. It is not necessary to stop a contraceptive injection if you are having an operation. However, it is always recommended that you tell the doctor that you are using the contraceptive injection.

How often do I need to see a doctor or nurse?
You only need to go to the clinic or your general practice when your injection is due. If you have *any* problems or want to ask any questions between injections, you should contact your doctor or nurse.

Chapter 4: The contraceptive implant

An implant is a small flexible rod that is placed just under your skin in your upper arm. It releases a progestogen hormone similar to the natural progesterone that women produce in their ovaries and works for up to three years.

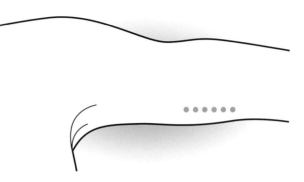

Myth busting

Myth: Implants move around the body
Truth: The implant stays under the skin of the upper arm where it is inserted.

Myth: The implant is less effective if you are overweight
Truth: The implant is suitable for most women regardless of their weight.

How effective is an implant?
The implant is over 99 per cent effective. Less than one woman in every 1,000 will get pregnant over three years. The implant is a long-acting reversible contraceptive. *All* long-acting methods are very effective because while they are being used you do not have to remember to take or use contraception.

How does an implant work?
The main way it works is to stop ovulation each month. It also:
- Thickens the mucus from your cervix. This makes it difficult for sperm to move through your cervix and reach an egg.
- Makes the endometrium thinner so it is less likely to accept a fertilised egg.

Where can I get an implant?
Only a doctor or nurse who has been trained to fit implants can insert the implant. You can go to a contraception or sexual health clinic or to the doctor or nurse at a general practice. All treatment is free and confidential.

Can anyone use an implant?

Most women can have an implant fitted. The doctor or nurse will need to ask you about your own and your family's medical history to make sure that the implant is suitable. You should tell them about any illnesses or operations you have had.

An implant **may** not be suitable for you if:
- you think you might already be pregnant
- you do not want your periods to change
- you take certain medicines.

You have now, or have had in the past:
- arterial disease or a history of serious heart disease or stroke
- thrombosis in any vein or artery
- active disease of the liver
- current breast cancer or breast cancer within the last five years
- unexplained vaginal bleeding (for example, bleeding between periods or after sex).

What are the advantages of an implant?
- It works for three years.
- It does not interrupt sex.
- You can use it if you are breastfeeding.
- Your fertility will return to normal as soon as the implant is taken out.
- It may reduce painful, heavy periods.

What are the disadvantages of an implant?
- Your periods may change in a way that is not acceptable to you (see *How will an implant affect my periods?* on page 47).
- Other side effects include acne in some women.
- Some women report having *temporary* side effects of tender breasts and changes in mood and sex drive.
- It is not suitable for women using enzyme inducing drugs (see *Can anything make an implant less effective?* on page 47).
- It requires a small procedure to fit and remove it.
- An implant does not protect you against sexually transmitted infections, so you may need to use condoms as well.

Are there any risks?

- Very rarely, soon after the implant is put in it can cause an infection in your arm, where it has been inserted.
- Research about the risk of breast cancer and hormonal contraception is complex and contradictory. Research suggests that women who use hormonal contraception appear to have a small increase in risk of being diagnosed with breast cancer compared to women who don't use hormonal contraception. Further research is ongoing.

When can I start using an implant?

You can have an implant fitted at any time in your menstrual cycle if it is certain that you are not pregnant. If the implant is put in during the first five days of your period you will be protected against pregnancy immediately.

If the implant is put in on any other day you will not be protected against pregnancy for the first seven days after it has been fitted. So you will need to use an additional method of contraception, such as condoms, during this time.

I've just had a baby. Can I use an implant?

You can have an implant put in three weeks (21 days) after you have given birth. If the implant is put in on or before day 21 you will be protected from pregnancy immediately. If the implant is put in later than day 21 you will need to use an additional method of contraception for seven days.

An implant can be used safely while you are breastfeeding and will not affect your milk supply.

Can I use an implant after a miscarriage or abortion?

The implant can be put in immediately after a miscarriage or abortion. You will be protected against pregnancy immediately.

How is an implant put in?

The implant, which is the size of a hair grip, is placed just under your skin in the inner area of your upper arm. A trained doctor or nurse will give you a local anaesthetic to numb

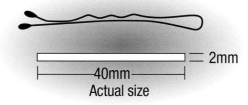

2mm
40mm
Actual size

the part of your arm where the implant will go so it won't hurt. It only takes a few minutes to put in and feels similar to having an injection. You won't need any stitches. After it has been fitted the doctor or nurse will check your arm to make sure that the implant is in position. You will also be shown how to feel the implant with your fingers, so you can check it is in place.

The area may be tender for a day or two and may be bruised and slightly swollen. The doctor or nurse will put a dressing on it to keep it clean and dry and to help stop the bruising. Keep this dressing on for a few days and try not to knock the area.

Don't worry about knocking the implant once the area has healed. It should not break or move around your arm. You will be able to do normal activities and move your arm.

You do not need to have a vaginal examination or cervical screening test to have an implant inserted.

How is an implant taken out?

An implant can be left in place for three years or it can be taken out sooner if you decide you want to stop using it. A specially trained doctor or nurse must take it out. The doctor or nurse will feel your arm to locate the implant and then give you a local anaesthetic injection in the area where the implant is. They will then make a tiny cut in your skin and gently pull the implant out. They will put a dressing on the arm to keep it clean and dry and to help stop the bruising. Keep this dressing on for a few days.

It usually only takes a few minutes to remove an implant. If the implant has been put in correctly, it should not be difficult to remove. Occasionally, an implant is difficult to feel under the skin and it may not be so easy to remove. If this happens you may be referred to a specialist centre to have it removed with the help of an ultrasound scan.

If you want to carry on using an implant, the doctor or nurse can put a new one in at the same time. You will continue to be protected against pregnancy.

Can anything make an implant less effective?

Some medicines may make an implant less effective. These include some of the medicines used to treat HIV, epilepsy and tuberculosis, and the complementary medicine St John's Wort. These are called enzyme inducing drugs. If you are using these medicines it will be recommended that you use additional contraception, such as condoms, or that you change your method of contraception. Always tell your doctor, nurse or dentist that you are using an implant if you are prescribed any medicines.

The implant is **not** affected by common antibiotics, diarrhoea or vomiting.

It is important to have your implant changed at the right time. If it is not, you will not be protected against pregnancy. If you have sex without using another method of contraception and don't wish to become pregnant you may want to consider using emergency contraception (see Chapter 17: Emergency contraception).

How will an implant affect my periods?

Your periods will probably change.

- In some women periods will stop completely.
- Some women will have irregular periods or spotting.
- Some women will have periods that last longer and or are heavier.

These changes may be a nuisance but they are not harmful. If you do have prolonged bleeding the doctor or nurse may be able to give you some additional hormone or medicine that can help control the bleeding. They may also check that the bleeding is not due to other causes, such as an infection.

What should I do if I want to stop using the implant or try to get pregnant?

If you want to stop using the implant you need to go back to the doctor or nurse and ask them to take it out. Your periods and normal fertility will return quickly and it is possible to get pregnant before you have your first period. If you don't wish to become pregnant then you should use another method of contraception from the day that your implant is removed.

If you want to try for a baby start pre-pregnancy care such as taking folic acid, stopping smoking and reducing how much alcohol you drink. You can ask your doctor or nurse for further advice.

If I go into hospital for an operation should I stop using the implant?
No. It is not necessary to stop using the implant if you are having an operation. However, it is always recommended that you tell the doctor that you are using the implant.

How long can I use the implant for?
If you have no medical problems you can continue to use the implant until you reach the menopause. Each implant will last for three years and will then need to be changed.

What should I do if I think that I'm pregnant?
The implant is a highly effective method of contraception. If you have not taken any medicine that might make the implant less effective and have had the implant changed on time it is very unlikely that you will become pregnant. If you think that you might be pregnant then do a pregnancy test or speak to your doctor or nurse as soon as possible. Using the implant will not affect a pregnancy test. If you do get pregnant while you are using the implant there is no evidence that it will harm the baby. The implant should be removed if you want to continue with the pregnancy.

How often do I need to see a doctor or nurse?
You only need to go to the clinic or your general practice if you have problems with your implant or when it needs to be replaced. If you have *any* problems, questions or want the implant removed you should contact your doctor or nurse.

Chapter 5: The intrauterine system (IUS)

An IUS is a small T-shaped plastic device which slowly releases a progestogen hormone. This is similar to the natural progesterone that women produce in their ovaries. A trained doctor or nurse will put the IUS into your uterus. The IUS has two soft threads at one end which hang through the cervix into the top of your vagina. The IUS works for up to five years.

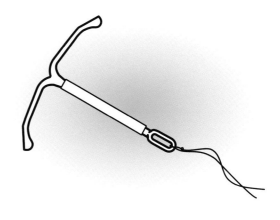

Myth busting

Myth: It can only be used by women who have already had a child
Truth: Most women, regardless of whether they have had children or not, can use the IUS.

Myth: The IUS causes abortions
Truth: The IUS works by stopping the sperm from meeting and fertilising the egg, by preventing the egg from implanting in the uterus and may stop ovulation. It does not cause an abortion.

Myth: It is huge
Truth: The IUS is T-shaped and measures 32mm horizontally and 32mm vertically. The threads are a little longer in order to hang out of your cervix, but usually are only a few centimetres long.

Q A How effective is an IUS?
The IUS is over 99 per cent effective. Less than one woman in every 100 women who use the IUS will get pregnant over five years. The IUS is a long-acting reversible contraceptive. *All* long-acting methods are very effective because while they are being used you do not have to remember to take or use contraception.

When will an IUS start to work?
The IUS can be fitted any time in your menstrual cycle if it is certain that you are not pregnant. If it is fitted in the first seven days of your menstrual cycle you will be immediately protected against pregnancy. If it is fitted at any other time, you will need to use additional contraception for the first seven days. If you have a short menstrual cycle with your period coming every 23 days or less, starting the IUS as late as the seventh day of your cycle may not provide you with immediate contraceptive protection. This is because you may ovulate early in your menstrual cycle. You may wish to talk to your doctor or nurse about this and whether you need to use additional contraception for the first seven days.

How does an IUS work?
- It makes the endometrium thinner so it is less likely to accept a fertilised egg.
- It also thickens the mucus from your cervix. This makes it difficult for sperm to move through it and reach an egg.
- In some women it stops ovulation but most women who use an IUS continue to ovulate.

What are the advantages of an IUS?
- It works for five years.
- It doesn't interrupt sex.
- Your periods usually become much lighter and shorter, and sometimes less painful. They may stop completely after the first year of use. An IUS can be useful if you have heavy, painful periods.
- It can be used if you are breastfeeding.
- Your fertility will return to normal when the IUS is removed.
- It is useful if you cannot use estrogens, like those found in the combined pill.
- The IUS is not affected by other medicines.

What are the disadvantages of an IUS?
- Your periods may change in a way that is not acceptable to you (see *Will an IUS affect my periods?* on page 54).
- Some women report having acne, headaches and breast tenderness.
- Some women develop small fluid-filled cysts on their ovaries. These are not dangerous and do not usually need to be treated. Often there are no symptoms, but some women may have pelvic pain. These cysts usually disappear without treatment.
- An IUS does not protect you against sexually transmitted infections, so you may need to use condoms as well. If you get an infection when the IUS is in place this could lead to pelvic infection if it is not treated.

Are there any risks?
- There is a very small chance of you getting an infection during the first 20 days after an IUS is put in. You may be advised to have a check for any existing infection before an IUS is fitted.
- The IUS can be pushed out by your uterus (expulsion) or it can move (displacement). This is not common and is more likely to happen soon after it has been put in and you may not know it has happened. This is why your doctor or nurse will teach you how to check your IUS threads every month.
- It is not common, but there is a risk that an IUS might go through (perforate) your uterus or cervix when it is put in. This may cause pain, but often there are no symptoms. If this happens, the IUS may have to be removed by surgery. The risk is low when an IUS is fitted by an experienced doctor or nurse.
- If you do become pregnant while you are using the IUS there is a small risk of ectopic pregnancy. The risk of ectopic pregnancy is less in women using an IUS than in women using no contraception.

Can anyone use an IUS?
Most women can use an IUS, including women who have never been pregnant and women who are HIV positive. Your doctor or nurse will need to ask you about your own and your family's medical history. Do mention any illness or operations you have had as some may require specialist care when the IUS is fitted. Some of the conditions which **may** mean you should not use an IUS are:
- you think you might already be pregnant
- you or a partner are at risk of getting a sexually transmitted infection.

You have now or had in the past:

- current breast cancer or breast cancer within the last five years
- current cervical cancer
- active disease of the liver
- unexplained bleeding from your vagina (for example between periods or after sex)
- current arterial disease or history of serious heart disease or stroke
- current thrombosis in any vein or artery
- an untreated sexually transmitted infection or pelvic infection
- problems with your uterus or cervix.

If you are aged 45 or older when the IUS is fitted, it can be left in until the menopause or until contraception is no longer needed.

I've just had a baby. Can I use an IUS?
An IUS is usually put in from four weeks after a vaginal or caesarean birth. You will need to use another method of contraception from three weeks (day 21) after the birth until the IUS is put in. You will need to use additional contraception for the first seven days. It can also be put in within 48 hours of birth. An IUS can be used safely while you are breastfeeding and will not affect your milk supply.

Can I use an IUS after a miscarriage or abortion?
An IUS can be put in by an experienced doctor or nurse immediately after a miscarriage or abortion. You will be protected against pregnancy immediately.

Where can I get an IUS?
You can go to a contraception or sexual health clinic. Some doctors and practice nurses at your general practice will fit an IUS.

How is an IUS put in?
The IUS is fitted inside the uterus by a trained doctor or nurse. They will examine you internally to find the position and size of your uterus before they put in an IUS. Sometimes they will check for any existing infection. It is best to do this before the IUS is put in. Sometimes you may be given antibiotics at the same time as the IUS is fitted.

Fitting an IUS takes about 15–20 minutes. It can be uncomfortable or painful for some women, and you might want to use pain relieving drugs or local anaesthetic.

Your doctor or nurse should talk to you about this beforehand. You may get period-type pain after the IUS is fitted. Pain relieving drugs can help with this.

What if I feel unwell after the IUS is put in?

If you feel unwell and have any pain in your lower abdomen, with a high temperature or a smelly discharge from your vagina in the first three weeks after the IUS is fitted, see a doctor or go back to the clinic where it was fitted **as soon as possible**. You may have an infection.

How will I know the IUS is still in place?

An IUS has two threads attached to the end that hang a little way down through your cervix into the top of your vagina. The doctor or nurse will teach you to feel for the threads to make sure the IUS is still in place. You should do this a few times in the first month and then after each period or at regular intervals.

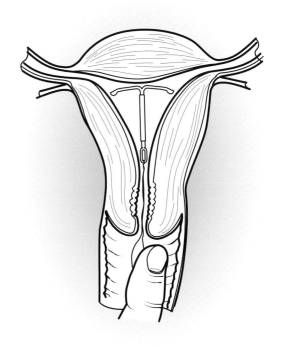

It is very unlikely that an IUS will come out, but if you cannot feel the threads or if you think you can feel the IUS itself, you may not be protected against pregnancy. Use additional contraception, such as condoms and see your doctor or nurse straightaway. If you had sex recently you might need to use emergency contraception (see Chapter 17: Emergency contraception).

Rarely, a partner may say he can feel the threads during sex. If this is the case, get your doctor or nurse to check the threads.

Is it safe to use tampons if I have an IUS fitted?

Yes, you can use tampons or towels.

When can the IUS be removed?

A trained doctor or nurse can take out the IUS at any time by pulling gently on the threads. If you are not going to have another IUS put in, and you don't want to become pregnant, use additional contraception, such as condoms, for seven days before the IUS is taken out. This is to stop sperm getting into your body. Sperm can live for up to seven days inside your body, and could fertilise an egg once the IUS is removed. Your normal fertility returns quickly after the IUS is taken out.

If you want to try for a baby start pre-pregnancy care such as taking folic acid, stopping smoking and reducing how much alcohol you drink. You can ask your doctor or nurse for advice.

Will an IUS affect my periods?

Yes. In the first six months it is common to have irregular bleeding or spotting, Periods may become lighter than usual or may continue to be irregular and many women find that their periods stop altogether. If this happens to you, do not worry as it is perfectly healthy.

What if I become pregnant while I am using the IUS?

Very few women become pregnant while using an IUS. If you do become pregnant there is a small increased risk of you having an ectopic pregnancy. An ectopic pregnancy develops outside your uterus, usually in a fallopian tube. If you think you might be pregnant or have a sudden or unusual pain in your lower abdomen, seek medical advice as soon as possible. This might be the warning sign of an ectopic pregnancy.

If you are pregnant, the IUS should be removed as soon as possible, whether or not you wish to continue with the pregnancy. If you want to continue with the pregnancy, removing the IUS can increase the risk of miscarriage.

How often do I need to see a doctor or nurse?

You need to have your IUS checked by a doctor or nurse 3–6 weeks after it is put in. The IUS can stay in for five years, or longer if you are over 45 years old. If you have *any* problems, questions or want the IUS removed you can go and see your doctor or nurse at any time.

Chapter 6: The intrauterine device (IUD)

An IUD is a small plastic and copper device that is put into your uterus. It has one or two soft threads on the end. These thin threads hang through the cervix into the top of your vagina. An IUD can stay in for 5–10 years, depending on type. There are different types and sizes of IUD to suit different women. An IUD is sometimes called a 'coil'.

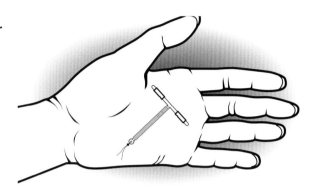

Myth busting

- **Myth: It can only be used by women who have already had a child**
- **Truth:** Most women, regardless of whether they have had children or not, can use the IUD.

- **Myth: An IUD causes an abortion**
- **Truth:** An IUD does not cause an abortion. It works by stopping the sperm from meeting and fertilising the egg and by preventing the egg from implanting in the uterus.

- **Myth: It is huge**
- **Truth:** An IUD is generally a T-shaped or straight plastic device. It is small enough to fit inside your uterus and is roughly the size of a matchstick.

- **Myth: The IUD makes you infertile**
- **Truth:** The IUD does not make you infertile. When you stop using it, your fertility will return to normal.

How effective is an IUD?
There are different types of IUD. Newer IUDs contain more copper and are the most effective – over 99 per cent effective. This means less than two women in 100 will get pregnant over five years. Older IUDs have less copper and are less effective. The IUD is a long-acting reversible contraceptive. *All* long-acting methods are very effective because while they are being used you do not have to remember to take or use contraception.

When will the IUD start to work?
An IUD can be put in at any time in your menstrual cycle if it is certain that you are not pregnant. It will be effective immediately.

How does an IUD work?
The main way an IUD works is to stop sperm reaching an egg. It does this by preventing sperm from surviving in the cervix, uterus or fallopian tube. It may also work by stopping a fertilised egg from implanting in the uterus.

What are the advantages of an IUD?
- It works as soon as it is put in.
- It works for 5–10 years depending on type.
- It doesn't interrupt sex.
- It can be used if you are breastfeeding.
- Your fertility returns to normal as soon as the IUD is taken out.
- It is not affected by other medicines.

What are the disadvantages of an IUD?
- Your periods may be heavier, longer or more painful. This may improve after a few months.
- You will first need an internal examination to check it is suitable for you to use and another when it is fitted.
- The IUD does not protect you from sexually transmitted infections so you may have to use condoms as well. If you get an infection when an IUD is in place this could lead to a pelvic infection if it is not treated.

Are there any risks?

- There is a very small chance of you getting an infection during the first 20 days after an IUD is put in. You may be advised to have a check for any existing infection before an IUD is fitted.
- The IUD can be pushed out by your uterus (expulsion) or it can move (displacement). This is not common. This is more likely to happen soon after it has been put in and you may not know it has happened. This is why your doctor or nurse will teach you how to check your IUD threads every month.
- It is not common, but there is a risk that an IUD might go through (perforate) your uterus or cervix when it is put in. This may cause pain but often there are no symptoms. If it happens, the IUD may have to be removed by surgery. The risk of perforation is low when an IUD is fitted by an experienced doctor or nurse.
- If you do become pregnant while you are using an IUD there is a small increased risk of you having an ectopic pregnancy (see *What if I become pregnant while I am using an IUD?* on page 60).The risk of ectopic pregnancy is less in women using an IUD than in women using no contraception at all.

Can anyone use an IUD?

Most women can use an IUD, including women who have never been pregnant and women who are HIV positive. Your doctor or nurse will need to ask you about your medical history to check if the IUD is suitable for you. Do mention any illness or operations which you have had as some may require specialist care when the IUD is fitted. Some of the conditions which **may** mean you should not use an IUD are:

- you think you might already be pregnant
- you or a partner are at risk of getting a sexually transmitted infection.

You have:

- an untreated sexually transmitted infection or pelvic infection
- problems with your uterus or cervix
- unexplained bleeding from your vagina (for example, between periods or after sex)
- current thrombosis
- current cervical cancer.

If you are aged 40 or older when the IUD is fitted, it can be left in until the menopause.

I've just had a baby. Can I use an IUD?
An IUD is usually put in from four weeks after a vaginal or caesarean birth. You will need to use another method of contraception from three weeks (day 21) after the birth until the IUD is put in. It can also be put in within 48 hours of birth. You will be protected from pregnancy immediately.

An IUD can be used safely while you are breastfeeding and will not affect your milk supply.

Can I use an IUD after a miscarriage or abortion?
An IUD can be put in immediately after a miscarriage or abortion. You will be protected against pregnancy immediately.

Where can I get an IUD?
You can go to a contraception or sexual health clinic or to a doctor or nurse at a general practice. Some doctors and practice nurses will fit an IUD, but not all.

How is an IUD put in?
The IUD is put inside the uterus. The doctor or nurse will examine you internally to find the position and size of your uterus before they put in an IUD. Sometimes they will check for any existing infection. It is best to do this before the IUD is put in. In some circumstances you may be given antibiotics at the same time as the IUD is fitted.

Fitting an IUD takes about 15–20 minutes. It can be uncomfortable or painful for some women, and you might want to use a local anaesthetic. Your doctor or nurse should talk to you about this beforehand. You may get a period-type pain and some light bleeding for a few days after the IUD is fitted. Pain relieving drugs can help with this.

What if I feel unwell after the IUD is put in?
If you feel unwell and have any pain in your lower abdomen, with a high temperature or a smelly discharge from your vagina in the first three weeks after the IUD is fitted, see a doctor or go back to the clinic where it was fitted **as soon as possible**. This is because you may have an infection.

How will I know that the IUD is still in place?

An IUD has one or two threads attached to the end that hang a little way through your cervix into the top of your vagina. The doctor or nurse will teach you how to feel the threads to make sure the IUD is still in place. You should do this a few times in the first month and then after each period or at regular intervals. It is very unlikely that an IUD will come out, but if you cannot feel the threads, or if you think you can feel the IUD itself, you may not be protected against pregnancy. See your doctor or nurse straightaway and use additional contraception, such as condoms. If you had sex recently you might need to use emergency contraception (see Chapter 17: Emergency contraception).

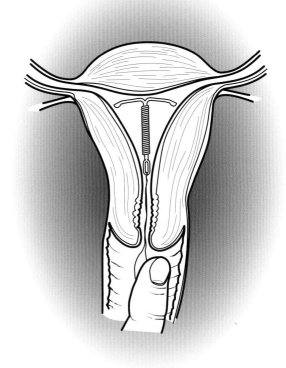

Rarely, a partner may say he can feel the threads during sex. If this is the case, get your doctor or nurse to check the threads.

Is it safe to use tampons if I have an IUD fitted?

Yes, you can use tampons or towels.

When can the IUD be removed?

A trained doctor or nurse can take the IUD out at any time, by pulling gently on the threads. If you are not going to have another IUD put in, and you don't want to become pregnant, use additional contraception, such as condoms, for seven days before the IUD is taken out. This is to stop sperm getting into your body. Sperm can live for up to seven days inside your body and could cause a pregnancy once the IUD is removed. Your fertility returns to normal as soon as the IUD is taken out.

If you want to try for a baby start pre-pregnancy care such as taking folic acid, stopping smoking and reducing how much alcohol you drink. You can ask your doctor or nurse for advice.

Will an IUD affect my periods?

You may have some light bleeding between your periods in the first six months after you have had the IUD fitted. Many women have heavier, longer and more painful periods. This may improve over time. If you have prolonged bleeding it may be possible for the doctor or nurse to give you hormones or medicine that can help control the bleeding. They may also check the bleeding is not due to other causes such as infection.

You may wish to consider using a hormone releasing IUD – an intrauterine system (IUS) – which will reduce bleeding and pain.

What if I become pregnant while I am using an IUD?

Very few women become pregnant while using an IUD. If you do become pregnant there is a small increased risk of having an ectopic pregnancy. An ectopic pregnancy develops outside the uterus, usually in a fallopian tube. If you think you might be pregnant or have a sudden or unusual pain in your lower abdomen, seek medical advice as soon as possible. This might be the warning sign of an ectopic pregnancy.

If you are pregnant the IUD should be removed as soon as possible, whether or not you wish to continue with the pregnancy. If you want to continue with the pregnancy, removing the IUD can increase the risk of miscarriage.

How often do I need to see a doctor or nurse?

You should have your IUD checked 3–6 weeks after it is put in. An IUD can stay in for 5–10 years, depending on type, or longer if you have it put in over the age of 40. Do contact your doctor or nurse if you have *any* problems, questions or want it removed.

Chapter 7: Female sterilisation

Both male and female sterilisation work by stopping the egg and the sperm meeting. In female sterilisation this is done by cutting, sealing or blocking the fallopian tubes.

Female sterilisation is a permanent method of contraception, suitable for people who are sure they never want children or do not want more children. You may want to find out about long-acting reversible contraceptives which are as effective as female sterilisation, but reversible. See Chapters 3–6 on the contraceptive implant, contraceptive injections, IUS and IUD, speak to a doctor or nurse or contact FPA (see Chapter 22: Useful organisations).

Myth busting

Myth: You do not feel sexy after female sterilisation
Truth: A woman may not feel sexy at different times in her life for many different reasons and may have a mixture of emotions after female sterilisation. This is normal. However, female sterilisation does not effect hormones and there is no reason why a woman should not feel sexy again after female sterilisation. Her sex drive and enjoyment of sex should not be affected. For many women it is improved, as they no longer fear an unplanned pregnancy.

Myth: It involves having your uterus and/or ovaries removed
Truth: Female sterilisation only affects your fallopian tubes, which are cut, sealed or blocked.

What is female sterilisation?
Your fallopian tubes are cut, sealed or blocked by an operation. This stops an egg and sperm meeting. Your ovaries, uterus and cervix are left in place so you will still ovulate each month but the egg is absorbed by your body.

How effective is female sterilisation?
The overall failure rate of female sterilisation is about one in 200. Research suggests that when it is done using a type of clip known as the Filshie clip, the failure rate in the ten years after the operation may be lower (one in 333–500).

There is a risk that female sterilisation will not work. The fallopian tubes, which carry the eggs, can rejoin. This can happen immediately or some years after the operation has been carried out.

What are the advantages of female sterilisation?
- It does not interrupt sex.
- You don't have to do anything about contraception ever again.

What are the disadvantages of female sterilisation?
- The tubes may rejoin and you will be fertile again. This is not common.
- It cannot be easily reversed.
- It does not protect you against sexually transmitted infections.

Can any woman be sterilised?
Sterilisation is for women who are sure they do not want more children or any children. You should not decide to be sterilised if you or your partner are not completely sure or if you are under any stress, for example after a birth, miscarriage, abortion or family or relationship crisis.

Research shows that more women regret sterilisation if they were sterilised when they were under 30 years old; had no children; or were not in a relationship. Because of this, young or single people may receive extra counselling.

Where can I go for advice on female sterilisation?
You can go to your general practice or to a contraception or sexual health clinic. If you prefer not to go to your own general practice, or they don't provide contraceptive services, they will refer you to another practice or clinic. All treatment is confidential and **free**. In some areas, NHS waiting lists for female sterilisation can be quite long. You can pay to have the operation done privately.

What information should I receive before I decide to be sterilised?
You should get full information and counselling if you want to be sterilised. This gives you a chance to talk about the operation in detail and any concerns you may have. You should be told about:

- other highly effective long-acting reversible contraceptives
- female sterilisation, its failure rate, any possible complications and reversal difficulties.

Anyone being sterilised will have to sign a consent form.

Do I need my partner's permission?
By law you do not need your partner's permission but some doctors prefer both partners to agree to the operation after information and counselling.

Can female sterilisation be reversed?
Female sterilisation is meant to be permanent. There are reversal operations for some methods but they are not always successful. The success will depend upon how and when you were sterilised. Reversal is rarely available on the NHS and can be difficult and expensive to obtain privately.

How is female sterilisation done?
There are several ways of blocking the fallopian tubes: tying, cutting and removing a small piece of the tube, sealing, or applying clips or rings. There are two main ways of reaching the fallopian tubes – laparoscopy or mini-laparotomy.

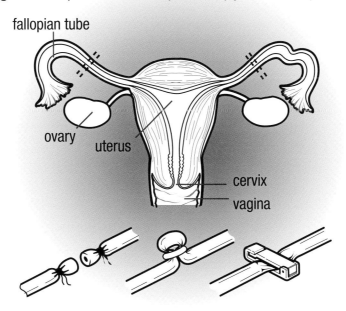

fallopian tube

ovary

uterus

cervix

vagina

Laparoscopy is the most common method. You should be told which method is being used and why it has been chosen. You will be given a general anaesthetic, or possibly a local anaesthetic. A doctor will make two tiny cuts, one just below your navel and the other just above the bikini line. They will then insert a laparoscope, which lets the doctor clearly see your reproductive organs. The doctor will seal or block your fallopian tubes, usually with clips or occasionally with rings.

For a mini-laparotomy you will usually have a general anaesthetic and spend a couple of days in hospital. The doctor will make a small cut in your abdomen, usually just below the bikini line, to reach your fallopian tubes. The time you stay in hospital after sterilisation depends on the anaesthetic and the method used. It can be as little as one day.

Hysteroscopic sterilisation is a new method and does not involve making any cuts. A tiny titanium (metal) coil is inserted into the fallopian tubes through the vagina and cervix. Body tissue grows around the coil and blocks the fallopian tube. This can be done under local anaesthetic or heavy sedation. This method is *not* reversible. Alternative contraception needs to be used after this procedure for at least three months. You will then need a test to check that the fallopian tubes are blocked. This method may not yet be widely available. The doctor will discuss your options with you.

How will I feel after the operation?
If you have a general anaesthetic you may feel unwell and a little uncomfortable for a few days. This is not unusual, and you may have to take things easy for a week or so. You may have some slight bleeding from your vagina, and pain. If this gets worse, see your doctor. Your doctor should tell you how the operation was done, if there were any complications and how to look after yourself.

How will female sterilisation affect my periods?
Your periods will continue to be as regular as they were before sterilisation. Occasionally, some women find that their periods become heavier. This is usually because they have stopped using hormonal contraception, which may have lightened their periods previously.

Are there any serious risks or complications?
If female sterilisation fails, and you do become pregnant, there is a small increased risk of ectopic pregnancy. This develops outside your uterus, usually in

the fallopian tube. Although this is not common, it is dangerous. You should seek advice straightaway if you think you might be pregnant or have a light or delayed period, unusual vaginal bleeding, or if you have sudden or unusual pain in your lower abdomen.

All operations carry some risk, but the risk of serious complications is low. Information on anaesthetics is provided by the Royal College of Anaesthetists (see Chapter 22: Useful organisations).

When is female sterilisation effective?
You will need to use contraception until your operation **and** for four weeks afterwards. If you have been sterilised using the hysteroscopic method you will need to use contraception for at least three months. You can have sex as soon as it's comfortable.

Chapter 8: Male sterilisation

Both male and female sterilisation work by stopping the egg and the sperm meeting. In male sterilisation, this is done by cutting and sealing or tying the vas deferens. It is sometimes called a vasectomy.

Male sterilisation is a permanent method, suitable for people who are sure they never want children or do not want more children. You may want to find out about other long-acting reversible contraceptives which are as effective as male sterilisation, but reversible. See Chapters 3–6 on the contraceptive implant, contraceptive injections, IUS and IUD, speak to a doctor or nurse or contact FPA (see Chapter 22: Useful organisations).

Myth busting

- **Myth: Male sterilisation is the same as castration**
  Truth: Castration is removal of the testicles. Male sterilisation only affects your vas deferens, which are cut and sealed or tied.

- **Myth: You can tell by looking at a man that he's been sterilised**
  Truth: Male sterilisation will not change a man's physical appearance in any way.

- **Myth: Sterilised men have higher voices**
  Truth: Male sterilisation cannot alter your voice.

- **Myth: Male sterilisation will put a man off sex**
  Truth: A man may not feel like sex at different times in his life, for many different reasons, and he may have a mixture of emotions after male sterilisation. This is normal. However, male sterilisation does not affect hormones and there is no reason why a man should not feel like sex again after sterilisation. His sex drive and enjoyment of sex should not be affected. For many men it is improved, as they no longer fear an unplanned pregnancy.

What is male sterilisation?
The vas deferens that carries sperm
from your testicles to your penis is
cut and sealed or tied.

 How effective is male sterilisation?
About one in 2,000 male sterilisations
fail.

There is a risk that male sterilisation
will not work. The tube that carries the
sperm can rejoin after sterilisation. This
can happen immediately or some years
after the operation has been carried out.
So if the partner of a sterilised man ever
thinks she might be pregnant, she
should see a doctor or nurse as soon as possible.

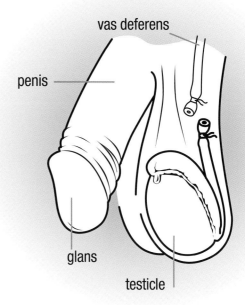

vas deferens

penis

glans

testicle

What are the advantages of male sterilisation?
- It does not interrupt sex.
- You don't have to do anything about contraception ever again.

What are the disadvantages of male sterilisation?
- The tubes may rejoin and you will be fertile again. This is not common.
- It cannot be easily reversed.
- It does not protect you against sexually transmitted infections.
- It takes at least two months for it to be effective.

 Can any man be sterilised?
Sterilisation is for men who are sure they do not want more children or any
children. You should not decide to be sterilised if you or your partner are not
completely sure or if you are under any stress, for example after a birth,
miscarriage, abortion or family or relationship crisis.

Research shows that more men regret sterilisation if they were sterilised when they were under 30 years old, had no children or were not in a relationship. Because of this, young or single people may receive extra counselling.

Where can I go for advice on male sterilisation?

You can go to your general practice or to a contraception or sexual health clinic. If you prefer not to go to your own general practice, or they don't provide contraceptive services, they will refer you to another practice or clinic. All treatment is confidential and **free**. In some areas, NHS waiting lists for male sterilisation can be quite long. You can pay to have the operation done privately.

What information should I receive before I decide to be sterilised?

You should get full information and counselling if you want to be sterilised. This gives you a chance to talk about the operation in detail and any concerns you may have. You should be told about:

- other highly effective long-acting reversible contraceptives
- male sterilisation, its failure rate, any possible complications and reversal difficulties.

Anyone being sterilised will have to sign a consent form.

Do I need my partner's permission?

By law you do not need your partner's permission but some doctors prefer both partners to agree to the operation after information and counselling.

Can male sterilisation be reversed?

Male sterilisation is meant to be permanent. There are reversal operations but they are not always successful. The success will depend upon how and when you were sterilised. Reversal is rarely available on the NHS and can be difficult and expensive to obtain privately.

How is male sterilisation done?

You will be given a local anaesthetic. To reach the vas deferens the doctor will make either a small cut or puncture, known as the no-scalpel method, in the skin of your scrotum. The doctor will then cut the tube and close the ends by tying them or sealing them with heat. Sometimes a small piece of the tube is removed when they are cut. The opening(s) in your scrotum will be very small and you may not need to have any stitches afterwards. If you do, dissolvable stitches or surgical tape will be used.

The operation takes about 10–15 minutes and may be done in a clinic, hospital outpatient department or some general practice settings. Sometimes it is necessary to do the operation using a general anaesthetic, but this is not common.

How will I feel after the operation?

Your scrotum may become bruised, swollen and painful. Wearing tight-fitting underpants, to support your scrotum, day and night for a week may help. You should avoid strenuous exercise for at least a week. For most men the pain is quite mild and they do not need any further help. The doctor or nurse should give you information about how to look after yourself.

Are there any serious risks or complications?

Research shows that there are no known serious long-term health risks caused by male sterilisation.

Occasionally, some men have bleeding, a large swelling, or an infection. In this case, see your doctor as soon as possible. Sometimes sperm may leak out of the tube and collect in the surrounding tissue. This may cause inflammation and pain immediately or a few weeks, or months later. If this happens it can be treated. Some men may experience ongoing pain in their testicles. This is known as chronic pain. Treatment for this is often unsuccessful.

The large majority of men having a sterilisation will have a local anaesthetic but sometimes a general anaesthetic is used. All operations using a general anaesthetic carry some risks, but serious problems are rare. Information on anaesthetics is provided by the Royal College of Anaesthetists (see Chapter 22: Useful organisations).

When will male sterilisation be effective?

You need to use an additional method of contraception after the operation because sperm are left in the tubes that lead to the penis. The rate these sperm are used up varies from man to man. About eight weeks after the operation, you should have a semen test to see if the sperm have gone. Sometimes more than one test is needed. You can have sex as soon as it is comfortable, but **you can only rely on male sterilisation for contraception after you have been told that the semen test is negative**.

Chapter 9: The contraceptive patch

The contraceptive patch is a small, thin, beige coloured patch, nearly 5cm x 5cm in size. You stick it on your skin and it releases two hormones – estrogen and progestogen. These are similar to the natural hormones that women produce in their ovaries and are like those used in the combined pill and contraceptive vaginal ring.

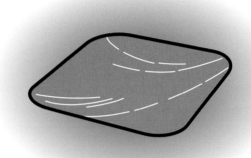

Myth busting

Myth: It's a relatively new method so we don't know a lot about it
Truth: All new methods of contraception go through rigorous and extensive tests to check their safety.

Myth: The patch will come off easily or it will get stuck to a partner
Truth: The patch is *very* sticky and should stay on. It should not come off in the shower, bath, hot tub or sauna, or during exercise. Therefore, it is unlikely to get stuck to a partner.

Myth: It will cause an allergic reaction like plasters
Truth: Some people who suffer an allergic reaction, such as a rash, when they use plasters may find that they have the same reaction to the contraceptive patch. However, this is unlikely to affect most people.

How effective is the patch?
If used correctly and according to instructions the patch is over 99 per cent effective. This means less than one woman in 100 will get pregnant in a year. If the patch is **not** used according to instructions, more women will become pregnant. Research has shown that the patch may not be so effective for women who weigh 90kg (14 stone or over).

How does the patch work?

The patch releases a daily dose of hormones through the skin, into the bloodstream. It works in the same way as the combined pill. The main way it works is to stop ovulation. It also:

- Thickens the mucus from your cervix. This makes it difficult for sperm to move through it and reach an egg.
- Makes the endometrium thinner so it is less likely to accept a fertilised egg.

Where can I get the patch?

You can go to a contraception or sexual health clinic, or general practice. If you prefer not to go to your own general practice, or they don't provide contraceptive services, they can give you information about another practice or clinic. All treatment is free and confidential. You don't need to have a vaginal or breast examination or cervical screening test when you are first prescribed the patch.

Can anyone use the patch?

Not everyone can use the patch so your doctor or nurse will need to ask you about your own and your family's medical history to make sure the patch is suitable. Do mention any illnesses or operations you have had. Some of the conditions which **may** mean you should not use the patch are:

- you think you might already be pregnant
- you smoke **and** are 35 years old or over
- you are 35 years old or over and stopped smoking less than a year ago
- you are very overweight
- you take certain medicines.

You have now or had in the past:

- thrombosis in any vein or artery
- a heart abnormality or circulatory disease, including hypertension
- current breast cancer or breast cancer within the last five years
- very severe migraines or migraines with aura
- disease of the liver or gall bladder
- diabetes with complications or diabetes for more than 20 years.

If you are healthy, don't smoke and there are no medical reasons for you not to use the patch, you can use it until your menopause. Women using the patch will need to change to another method at the age of 50 years.

What are the advantages of the patch?

- You don't have to think about it every day – you only have to remember to replace the patch once a week.
- It doesn't interrupt sex and is easy to use.
- Unlike the pill, the hormones do not need to be absorbed by the stomach, so the patch is not affected if you vomit or have diarrhoea.
- It usually makes your bleeds regular, lighter and less painful.
- It may help with premenstrual symptoms.
- It may reduce the risk of cancer of the ovary, uterus and colon.
- It may reduce the risk of fibroids, ovarian cysts and non-cancerous breast disease.

What are the disadvantages of the patch?

There are some serious side effects of the patch (see *Are there any risks?* below). In addition:

- It can be seen.
- It may cause skin irritation in some women.
- It may increase your blood pressure.
- You may get *temporary* side effects when you first start using the patch, these should stop within a few months. They include headaches, nausea, breast tenderness and mood changes.
- Breakthrough bleeding and spotting are also common in the first few months of use. If you are using the patch correctly, this is nothing to worry about. You will still be protected against pregnancy.
- It does not protect you against sexually transmitted infections, so you may need to use condoms as well.

Are there any risks?

The patch can have some serious side effects, but these are not common. For most women the benefits of the patch outweigh the possible risks. All risks and benefits should be discussed with your doctor or nurse.

- A very small number of women may develop a venous thrombosis, an arterial thrombosis, heart attack or stroke. If you have ever had thrombosis, you should not use the patch.
- The risk of venous thrombosis is greatest during the first year that you use the

patch, if you smoke, you are very overweight, are immobile for long periods or use a wheelchair, have severe varicose veins or a member of your immediate family had a venous thrombosis before they were 45 years old.

- The risk of arterial thrombosis is greatest if you smoke, are diabetic, have hypertension, are very overweight, have migraines with aura, or a member of your immediate family had a heart attack or stroke before they were 45 years old.
- Research into the risk of breast cancer and hormonal contraception is complex and contradictory. Research suggests that users of all hormonal contraception appear to have a small increased risk of being diagnosed with breast cancer compared to non-users of hormonal contraception. Further research is ongoing.
- Research suggests that there is a small increase in the risk of developing cervical cancer with longer use of estrogen and progestogen hormonal contraception.
- Some research suggests a link between using estrogen and progestogen hormonal contraception and developing a very rare liver cancer.

See a doctor straightaway if you have any of the following:
- pain in the chest, including any sharp pain which is worse when you breathe in
- breathlessness
- you cough up blood
- painful swelling in your leg(s)
- weakness, numbness, or bad 'pins and needles' in an arm or leg
- severe stomach pains
- a bad fainting attack or you collapse
- unusual headaches or migraines that are worse than usual
- sudden problems with your speech or eyesight
- jaundice.

If you need to go into hospital for an operation or you have an accident which affects the movement of your legs, you should tell the doctor that you are taking the patch. The doctor will decide if you need to stop using the patch or need other treatment to reduce the risk of developing thrombosis.

Will I put on weight if I use the patch?
No. Research has not shown that women put on weight when they use the patch. However, some women may find their weight changes throughout their cycle due to fluid retention.

When can I start to use the patch?
You can start the patch anytime in your menstrual cycle if you are sure you are not pregnant. If you start the patch on the first day of your period you will be protected against pregnancy immediately. You can also start to use the patch up to and including the fifth day of your period and you will be protected from pregnancy immediately.

However, if you have a short menstrual cycle with your period coming every 23 days or less, starting the patch as late as the fifth day of your cycle may not provide you with immediate contraceptive protection. This is because you may ovulate early in the menstrual cycle. You may wish to talk to your doctor or nurse about whether you need to use additional contraception. If you start the patch at any other time in your menstrual cycle you will need to use another contraceptive method, such as condoms, for the first seven days of using the patch.

I've just had a baby. Can I use the patch?
You can start to use the patch from three weeks (21 days) after you gave birth if you are not breastfeeding. Starting on day 21 you will be protected against pregnancy straightaway. If you start later than day 21, you will need to use an additional method of contraception for seven days.

If you are breastfeeding a baby under six months old, using the patch may reduce your flow of milk. It is usually recommended that you use a different method of contraception.

Can I use the patch after a miscarriage or abortion?
You can start using the patch immediately after a miscarriage or abortion.
You will be protected from pregnancy straightaway.

| Week 1
1st Patch

Start day
Use patch for
seven days | Week 2
2nd Patch

Patch change day
Use patch for
seven days | Week 3
3rd Patch

Patch change day
Use patch for
seven days | Week 4
No Patch

**Do not apply
a patch**
This is your
patch-free week
(seven days) |

How do I use the patch?
You apply a new patch once a week, every week for three weeks (21 days).
You then stop using the patch for seven days (patch-free week). This is called
a patch cycle.

- **Week one:** You start the patch cycle by applying a new patch. This is known as the **start day**. Keep this patch on for seven days. Only use one patch at a time.
- **Week two:** Remove the patch and apply a new one immediately. This is known as the **change day**. This will be the same day of the week as the start day. The patch can be changed at any time of the day. Keep this patch on for seven days.
- **Week three:** Remove the patch and apply a new one immediately. Keep this patch on for seven days.
- **Patch-free week:** Remove the patch. You will now have seven days without using it. This is known as the **patch-free week**. During this week you may get a withdrawal bleed. This may not always happen – it is caused by you not taking hormones in the patch-free week. The bleeding can start at any time during the patch-free week. It is usually regular, lighter and less painful than a normal period.
- **New patch cycle:** After seven patch-free days you apply a new patch on the eighth day. You should do this even if you are still bleeding. This is now week one of a new patch cycle. Continue to use the patch as you did in the last

cycle, applying a new patch each week for three weeks. It is very important not to have more than seven days without using the patch or you may lose contraceptive protection (see *What if I forget to put on a new patch at the end of the patch-free week?* on page 78).

- **Disposing of the patch:** Used patches should be placed in the disposal sachet provided and put in a waste bin. They must not be flushed down the toilet.

 Where do I put the patch?

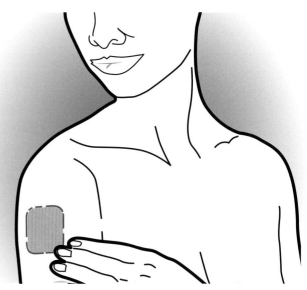

You can use the patch on most areas of your body as long as your skin is clean, dry and not very hairy. You should not put it on skin that is sore or irritated or anywhere that can be rubbed by tight clothing. Don't put it on your breasts. It is also a good idea to change the position of each new patch to help reduce the chance of any possible skin irritation.

 Am I protected from pregnancy during the seven day break?

Yes. You are protected if:

- you have used the previous three patches correctly **and**
- you start the patch cycle again on time **and**
- you are not taking other medicines that will affect the patch (see *If I take other medicines will it affect the patch?* on page 78).

 What if the patch falls off?

The patch is *very* sticky and should stay on. It should not come off in the shower, bath, hot tub or sauna, or during swimming or exercise. However, if it does come off, what you need to do will depend on how long it has been off.

Less than 48 hours

If the patch has been off for less than 48 hours:

- Reapply it as quickly as possible if it is still sticky.
- If it is not sticky it may not work so apply a new patch. Do not use a plaster or bandage to hold the old patch in place.

- You don't need to use any additional contraception and you are protected against pregnancy.
- Continue to use your patch as normal and change the patch on your normal change day.

48 hours or more

If the patch has been off for 48 hours or longer or you are unsure how long:

- Start a whole new patch cycle by applying a new patch as soon as possible. This is now week one of the patch cycle and you will now have a new day of the week as your start day and change day.
- Use another method of contraception for the next seven days.
- Ask your doctor or nurse for advice if you have had sex in the previous few days and were not using a condom as you may need emergency contraception.

What if I forget to take the patch off at the end of week one or week two?

Less than 48 hours

If the patch has been on for less than 48 hours:

- Take off the old patch and put on a new one.
- Continue to use your patch as normal, changing it on your normal change day.
- You don't need to use any additional contraception and you are protected against pregnancy.

48 hours or more

If the patch has been on for 48 hours or more:

- Start a whole new patch cycle by applying a new patch as soon as possible. This is now week one of the patch cycle and you will now have a new day of the week as your start day and change day.
- Use another method of contraception for the next seven days.
- Ask your doctor or nurse for advice if you have had sex in the previous few days and were not using a condom as you may need emergency contraception.

What if I forget to take the patch off at the end of week three?

Take the patch off as soon as you remember, have a patch-free break and start with a new patch on your **usual start day** even if you are bleeding. This means that you have a fewer number of patch-free days than usual. You will be protected against pregnancy and do not need to use any additional contraception. You may or may not bleed on the patch-free days.

What if I forget to put on a new patch at the end of the patch-free week?
This is the most risky time to forget to put on a patch. Put on a new patch as soon as you remember. This is now the beginning of your new patch cycle. You will now have a new day of the week as your start day and change day.

If you put on the new patch **48 hours or more after** your usual start day then you may not be protected from pregnancy. Use an additional method of contraception, such as condoms, for the next seven days. If you have had sex in the previous few days and were not using a condom ask your doctor or nurse for advice as you may need emergency contraception.

If I take other medicines will it affect the patch?
There are a few medicines that make the patch less effective. Ask your doctor, nurse or pharmacist for advice. Follow the instructions below if you are taking a medicine that affects the patch.

Common antibiotics – Continue using your patch as usual and use an additional method of contraception, such as condoms, while taking the antibiotics and for seven days after you've finished them. If you come to the end of your last patch week while still taking the antibiotics or still need to use additional contraception, then put on a new patch straightaway. Do not have your usual seven day break. You may or may not have a withdrawal bleed, this is normal.

If you are given antibiotics in the first patch week and you have had sex recently ask your doctor or nurse for advice as you may also need emergency contraception. If you take common antibiotics for more than two weeks, you will need to follow different instructions. Your doctor or nurse can advise you.

Some other medicines – These include some medicines used to treat epilepsy, HIV and TB, and the complementary medicine St John's Wort. These types of drugs are called enzyme inducers. If you take these medicines, talk to your doctor or nurse. It is often advised that you use a different method of contraception instead of the patch.

I am bleeding on days when I am using the patch, what should I do?
This is called breakthrough bleeding. It is very common when you first start using the patch. This is not harmful or anything to worry about. It may take up to three months to settle down. It is important to continue using the patch correctly, even if the bleeding is as heavy as your withdrawal bleed.

Bleeding may also be caused by not using the patch correctly or by a sexually transmitted infection. If it carries on or starts after you have used the patch for some time, then seek advice.

I didn't bleed in my patch-free week – am I pregnant?
If you have used all three patches correctly and have not taken any medicines which might have affected the patch, then it is very unlikely that you will be pregnant. Start your next patch at the right time. If you are worried ask your doctor or nurse for advice, or do a pregnancy test. Using the patch does not affect a pregnancy test. Always take a test or speak to a health professional if you miss more than one bleed. If you do become pregnant, there is no evidence to show that using the patch harms the baby.

Can I miss out a withdrawal bleed?
Yes. This is not harmful. To do this you just miss out the patch-free week by using another patch straightaway. Sometimes you do still get bleeding. This is nothing to worry about and if you are using the patch correctly, you will still be protected against pregnancy.

What should I do if I want to change to another method of contraception?
It is easy to change from the patch to another method of contraception. Talk to your doctor or nurse as you may need to miss out the patch-free week or use additional contraception for a short time.

What should I do if I want to stop using the patch or try to get pregnant?
Ideally, it is easier if you stop using the patch at the end of the patch cycle. If you don't want to wait until this time, ask your doctor or nurse for advice because you can risk becoming pregnant if you have had sex recently. If you do not want to become pregnant you should use another method of contraception as soon as you stop using the patch. Your normal periods may not come back immediately – for some women it can take a few months.

If you want to try for a baby it is advisable to wait for one natural period after stopping the patch before trying to get pregnant. This means the pregnancy can be dated more accurately and you can start pre-pregnancy care such as taking folic acid and stopping smoking. You can ask your doctor or nurse for advice. Don't worry if you get pregnant sooner, it will not harm the baby.

 Should I give my body a break from using the patch every few years or so?
No. You do not need to take a break because the hormones do not build up. There are no known benefits to your health or fertility from taking a break.

 Can I decorate the patch?
No. This is not recommended. You should also avoid covering the patch with body cream or lotions, such as sun tan lotion. This may cause the patch to become loose.

 How often do I need to see a doctor or nurse?
When you first start using the patch you will usually be given three months' supply to see how it suits you. After that you should go back to the doctor or nurse to get new supplies and to have your blood pressure checked. If there are no problems you can be given up to one year's supply of patches.

Chapter 10: The contraceptive vaginal ring

The contraceptive vaginal ring is a flexible, transparent, plastic ring. It is placed in the vagina where it releases two hormones – estrogen and progestogen. These are similar to the natural hormones that women produce in their ovaries and are like those used in the combined pill and the contraceptive patch.

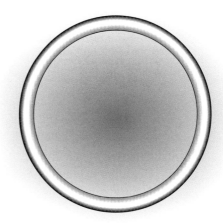

Myth busting

- **Myth: It's a relatively new method so we don't know a lot about it**
- **Truth:** All new methods of contraception go through rigorous and extensive tests to check their safety.

- **Myth: The ring dissolves over time so there is nothing left to remove**
- **Truth:** The ring is made of plastic and cannot dissolve. It should be removed from the vagina three weeks after it is put in.

- **Myth: There is not enough room for it in the vagina**
- **Truth:** There is room in the vagina for the ring – there is even room for a tampon and the ring at the same time.

- **Myth: My partner could taste or smell it and might be put off**
- **Truth:** The vaginal ring doesn't have a taste or a smell. Occasionally, it can be felt by a partner during sex but this is not unpleasant or uncomfortable for most people.

How effective is the vaginal ring?

If the vaginal ring is used correctly and according to instructions it is over 99 per cent effective. This means that less than one woman in 100 will get pregnant in a year. If the vaginal ring is **not** used according to instructions, more women will become pregnant.

How does the vaginal ring work?

The vaginal ring releases a constant dose of hormones into the bloodstream through the vaginal wall. The main way it works is to stop ovulation each month. It also:

- Thickens the mucus from your cervix. This makes it difficult for sperm to move through it and reach an egg.
- Makes the endometrium thinner so it is less likely to accept a fertilised egg.

Where can I get the vaginal ring?

You can go to a contraception or sexual health clinic or a general practice. If you prefer not to go to your own general practice, or if they don't provide contraceptive services, they can give you information about another practice or clinic. All treatment is free and confidential. You don't need to have a breast examination or cervical screening test when you are first prescribed the vaginal ring.

Can anyone use the vaginal ring?

Not everyone can use the vaginal ring so your doctor or nurse will need to ask you about your own and your family's medical history. Do mention any illnesses or operations you have had. Some of the conditions which **may** mean you should not use the vaginal ring are:

- you think you might be pregnant
- you smoke **and** are 35 years old or over
- you are 35 years old or older and stopped smoking less than a year ago
- you are very overweight
- you take certain medicines
- your vaginal muscles can't hold a vaginal ring.

You have now or had in the past:

- thrombosis in any vein or artery
- a heart abnormality or circulatory disease including hypertension
- current breast cancer or breast cancer within the last five years
- very severe migraines or migraines with aura
- active disease of the gall bladder or liver
- diabetes with complications or diabetes for more than 20 years
- unexplained bleeding from your vagina
- current cervical, ovarian, vaginal or uterine cancer.

If you are healthy, don't smoke and there are no medical reasons for you not to use the vaginal ring, you can use it until your menopause. Women using the vaginal ring will need to change to another method of contraception at the age of 50 years.

What are the advantages of the vaginal ring?
- You don't have to think about it every day – you only use one ring a month.
- It doesn't interrupt sex.
- It is easy to insert and remove.
- Unlike the pill, the hormones do not need to be absorbed by the stomach, so the ring is not affected if you vomit or have diarrhoea.
- Bleeding will usually become more regular, lighter and less painful.
- It may help with premenstrual symptoms.
- It may help reduce the risk of cancer of the ovary, uterus and colon.
- It may reduce the risk of fibroids, ovarian cysts and non-cancerous breast disease.

What are the disadvantages of the vaginal ring?
There are some serious side effects of the vaginal ring (see *Are there any risks?* below). In addition:
- Some women may not feel comfortable inserting and removing it.
- You may get *temporary* side effects at first including increased vaginal discharge and vaginal infections, headaches, nausea, breast tenderness and mood changes.
- Breakthrough bleeding and spotting may occur in the first few months of ring use (see *I am bleeding on the days when I am using the vaginal ring, what should I do?* on page 90).
- The vaginal ring does not protect you against sexually transmitted infections so you may need to use condoms as well.

Are there any risks?
The vaginal ring can have some serious side effects, but these are not common. For most women the benefits of using the ring outweigh the possible risks. All risks and benefits should be discussed with your doctor or nurse.
- A very small number of women may develop a venous thrombosis, an arterial

thrombosis or have a heart attack or stroke. If you have ever had thrombosis, you should not use the vaginal ring.

- The risk of venous thrombosis is greatest during the first year that you use the vaginal ring and if you smoke, you are very overweight, are immobile for a long period of time or use a wheelchair, have severe varicose veins or a member of your immediate family had a venous thrombosis before they were 45 years old.
- The risk of arterial thrombosis is greatest if any of the following apply to you: you smoke, are diabetic, have hypertension, are very overweight, have migraines with aura, or a member of your immediate family had a heart attack or stroke before they were 45 years old.
- Research into the risk of breast cancer and hormonal contraception is complex and contradictory. Research suggests that users of all hormonal contraception appear to have a small increased risk of being diagnosed with breast cancer compared to non-users of hormonal contraception. Further research is ongoing.
- Research suggests that there is a small increase in the risk of developing cervical cancer with longer use of estrogen and progestogen hormonal contraception.
- Some research suggests a link between using estrogen and progestogen hormonal contraception and developing a very rare liver cancer.

See a doctor straightaway if you have any of the following:
- pain in the chest, including any sharp pain which is worse when you breathe in
- breathlessness
- you cough up blood
- painful swelling in your leg(s)
- weakness, numbness, or bad pins and needles in an arm or leg
- severe stomach pains
- a bad fainting attack or you collapse
- unusual headaches or migraines that are worse than usual
- sudden problems with your speech or eyesight
- jaundice.

If you need to go into hospital for an operation or you have an accident which affects the movement of your legs, you should tell the doctor that you are using the vaginal ring. The doctor will decide if you need to stop using the ring or need other treatment to reduce the risk of developing thrombosis.

Will I put on weight if I use the vaginal ring?
No. Research has not shown that women put on weight when they use the vaginal ring. However, some women may find their weight changes throughout their cycle due to fluid retention.

When can I first start to use the vaginal ring?
If you did not use a hormonal contraceptive during your previous menstrual cycle and you are sure you are not pregnant, insert the vaginal ring on the first day of your period. You will be protected against pregnancy immediately. You can also start the ring on days 2–5 of your period but you must use additional contraception, such as condoms, for the first seven days you use the ring.

If you start the ring at any other time in your menstrual cycle you will also need to use additional contraception, such as condoms, for the first seven days.

If you are switching from another contraceptive method your doctor or nurse will advise you on when to start using the vaginal ring.

I've just had a baby. Can I use the vaginal ring?
If you feel comfortable you can start to use the vaginal ring three weeks (21 days) after you give birth if you are not breastfeeding. Starting on day 21 you will be protected from pregnancy immediately. If you start later than day 21 you will need to use additional contraception for the first seven days you use the ring.

If you are breastfeeding, the vaginal ring may reduce your flow of milk. It is usually recommended that you use a different method of contraception.

Can I use the vaginal ring after a miscarriage or abortion?
You can start to use the vaginal ring immediately after a miscarriage or abortion. You will be protected against pregnancy immediately.

How do I insert the vaginal ring?
Your doctor or nurse should advise you on how to insert and remove the vaginal ring. With clean hands squeeze the ring between your

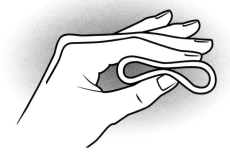

thumb and finger and use one hand to insert it into your vagina. If necessary, spread your labia with your other hand. Push the ring into your vagina until it feels comfortable. It does not need to cover your cervix to work.

 How will I know that the vaginal ring is in place?

The ring does not need to be in an exact position to work. Most women can't feel the ring. If you can feel it and it is also uncomfortable, push the ring a little further into your vagina. You can check it's still there with your fingers.

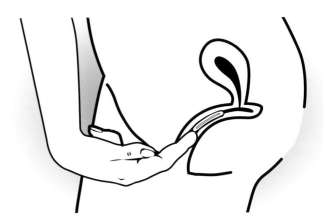

There is no danger that the vaginal ring can get lost inside the vagina – it is stopped by the cervix. However, if you are sure it's inside you but you can't feel it with your fingers, see a doctor or nurse.

 Will I, or my partner, be able to feel the vaginal ring during sex?

Occasionally you or a partner might be able to feel the ring during sex. This is not uncomfortable or unpleasant for most people. The ring is not likely to affect or harm your partner.

 How do I remove the ring?

Remove the vaginal ring by hooking a finger under it, or by grasping it between your thumb and finger and gently pulling it out. If you experience pain or bleeding when trying to remove the ring, or cannot remove it, tell your doctor or nurse immediately.

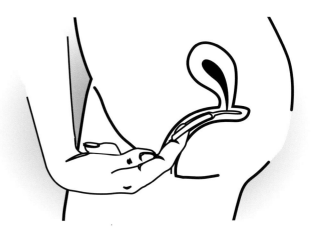

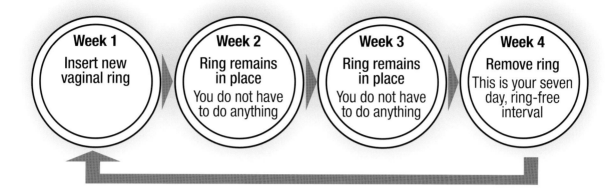

How do I use the vaginal ring?

- **Weeks 1–3:** The vaginal ring should be left in the vagina for three weeks (21 days). After three weeks remove the ring on the same day of the week that it was inserted.
- **Ring-free interval:** Stop using the ring for one week (seven days). This is known as the ring-free interval. During this week you may get a bleed. You don't have periods when you use the vaginal ring – you have a withdrawal bleed. This doesn't always happen and it is caused by you not taking hormones in the ring-free week.
- **New ring cycle:** After the ring-free interval, insert a new ring on the same day of the week that you took the previous one out. You should do this even if you are still bleeding. Continue using the ring as you did in the last cycle.
- **Disposing of the vaginal ring:** Put the used vaginal ring in the disposal sachet provided and place it in a waste bin. It must not be flushed down the toilet.

Am I protected from pregnancy during the seven day, ring-free interval?

Yes. You are protected if:

- you used the vaginal ring according to instructions during the last three weeks **and**
- you start the next ring cycle on time **and**
- you are not taking medicines that will affect the ring (see *If I take other medicines will it affect the vaginal ring?* on page 89).

What if I forget to take the vaginal ring out at the end of week three?

Seven days or less

If the ring has been left in for up to seven days after the end of week three (up to four weeks in total):

- As soon as you remember, remove the ring. Do not put another ring in. Start your seven day, ring-free interval. After the seven days insert a new ring on the same day of the week you removed it.

- You don't need to use additional contraception and you are protected against pregnancy.

More than seven days

If the ring has been left in for more than seven days after the end of week three (more than four weeks in total):

- As soon as you remember, remove the ring and insert a new ring immediately.
- You must use additional contraception until the new ring has been in place for seven continuous days.
- Ask your doctor or nurse for advice if you have had sex in the previous few days and were not using a condom as you may need emergency contraception.

What if I forget to put a new vaginal ring in at the end of the ring-free interval?

Insert a new ring as soon as you remember and use additional contraception until a new ring has been in place for seven continuous days. Ask your doctor or nurse for advice if you have had sex in the previous few days and were not using a condom as you may need emergency contraception.

Can the ring fall out of my vagina?

The muscles of your vagina hold the ring in place. Occasionally, however, the ring may come out of your vagina, for example if it wasn't inserted properly, during sex or a bowel movement (having a poo), or while removing a tampon. If this happens often, you may want to consider another method of contraception.

Research shows that the ring is not more likely to come out if you have had children.

What should I do if the ring comes out of my vagina for a short time?

The longer the ring has been out of the vagina, the higher the risk of pregnancy. You may also experience breakthrough bleeding. If the ring comes out of the vagina for:

Less than three hours:

- Rinse the ring with cool or lukewarm water and re-insert the same ring as soon as possible within three hours.
- You don't need to use additional contraception.

More than three hours in the first or second week of use:
- Rinse the ring with cool or lukewarm water and re-insert the same ring as soon as possible.
- You must use additional contraception until the ring has been in place for seven continuous days.
- Ask your doctor or nurse for advice if you have had sex in the previous few days and were not using a condom as you may need emergency contraception.

More than three hours in the third week of use:
Throw the ring away and choose one of the following two options:
1. insert a new ring immediately and start a new ring cycle. You may not experience a withdrawal bleed but breakthrough bleeding or spotting may occur, or
2. do not insert a new ring. Start your seven day, ring-free interval. You will have a withdrawal bleed. Insert a new ring seven days from the time the previous ring came out of the vagina. This option can only be chosen if the ring was used continuously for the previous seven days.

In both cases, you must use additional contraception until the ring has been in place for seven continuous days *and* ask your doctor or nurse for advice if you have had sex in the previous few days and were not using a condom as you may need emergency contraception.

If you lose the vaginal ring insert a new one and continue with the cycle that you were on.

What if the ring breaks inside my vagina?
This is very rare and it is unlikely to affect how the ring works. It will not harm you. Remove the broken ring and insert a new one as soon as possible. Continue with the cycle that you were on.

If I take other medicines will it affect the vaginal ring?
There are a few medicines that make the vaginal ring less effective. Ask your doctor, nurse or pharmacist for advice. Follow the instructions below if you are taking a medicine that affects the ring.

Common antibiotics – Continue using your ring as usual and use an additional method of contraception, such as condoms, while taking the antibiotics and for seven days after you've finished them. If you come to the start of your seven day, ring-free interval while still taking antibiotics or using additional contraception, insert a new ring immediately. Do not have your usual seven day ring-free interval. You may or may not have a withdrawal bleed, this is normal.

If you are given antibiotics in the first week of using your ring and you have had sex recently, ask your doctor or nurse for advice as you may also need to use emergency contraception. If you are taking a common antibiotic for more than two weeks, you will need to follow different instructions. Your doctor or nurse can advise you.

Some other medicines – These include some medicines used to treat epilepsy, HIV and TB, and the complementary medicine St John's Wort. These types of drugs are called enzyme inducers. If you take these medicines talk to your doctor or nurse. It is often advised that you use a different method of contraception instead of the vaginal ring. Treatments for thrush – do not affect the effectiveness of the ring.

I am bleeding on the days when I am using the vaginal ring, what should I do?
Breakthrough bleeding or spotting is common when you first start to use the vaginal ring and is not usually anything to worry about. It may take up to three months to settle down. It is important to continue using the ring correctly even if the bleeding is as heavy as your withdrawal bleed.

You can use a tampon while the ring is in place; this is not harmful. However, try to make sure that the ring does not come out accidentally when removing the tampon.

Bleeding may also be caused by not using the vaginal ring correctly or by a sexually transmitted infection. If it carries on or starts after you have used the ring for some time, seek advice.

I didn't bleed in my ring-free interval – am I pregnant?
If you used the ring according to instructions and have not taken any medicines that might have affected the ring (see *If I take other medications will it affect the vaginal ring?* on page 89), then it is very unlikely that you are pregnant. Start your next ring cycle at the right time. If you are worried ask your doctor or nurse for

advice or do a pregnancy test. Using the vaginal ring does not affect a pregnancy test. Always take a test or speak to a health professional if the ring has not been used properly, or if you miss more than one withdrawal bleed.

Can I miss out a withdrawal bleed?
Yes. This is not harmful. Remove the ring after three weeks and immediately insert another without having the seven day, ring-free interval. You may experience breakthrough bleeding but this is nothing to worry about. If you are using the ring correctly you will still be protected against pregnancy.

What should I do if I want to change to another method of contraception?
It is easy to change from the vaginal ring to another method of contraception. Get advice from your doctor or nurse. You may need to miss out the ring-free interval or use additional contraception.

What should I do if I want to stop using the vaginal ring or try to get pregnant?
Ideally, it is easier if you stop using the vaginal ring at the end of the ring cycle and do not insert a new ring after your withdrawal bleed. If you don't want to wait until this time, ask your doctor or nurse for advice because you can risk becoming pregnant if you have had sex recently. If you do not want to become pregnant you should use another method of contraception as soon as you stop using the ring. Your normal periods may not come back immediately – for some women it can take a few months.

If you want to try for a baby it is advisable to wait for one natural period after stopping the ring before trying to get pregnant. This means the pregnancy can be dated more accurately and you can start pre-pregnancy care such as taking folic acid and stopping smoking. You can ask your doctor or nurse for advice.

Should I give my body a break from the vaginal ring every few years or so?
No. You do not need to take a break because the hormones do not build up. There are no known benefits to your health or fertility from taking a break.

How often do I need to see a doctor or nurse?
When you first start using the vaginal ring you will be given a supply to see how it suits you. After that you should go back to the doctor or nurse to get new supplies and to have your blood pressure checked. If there are no problems, you can be given a further supply of vaginal rings.

Chapter 11: The combined pill

The combined pill is usually just called the pill. It contains two hormones – estrogen and progestogen. These are similar to the natural hormones women produce in their ovaries. There are a number of different combined pills. If you are taking a combined pill called Qlaira, some of the information in this chapter may not apply to you. Seek advice.

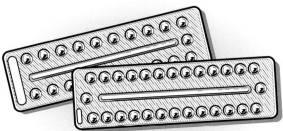

Myth busting

Myth: Using the combined pill makes you fat
Truth: Research has not shown that women put on weight when they use the combined pill. Some women may find that their weight changes throughout their cycle due to fluid retention. Some women may even lose weight when they use the combined pill.

Myth: Missing pills in the middle of the pack is riskiest
Truth: Starting a new pack of pills late or missing pills in the last week of the pack is riskier.

Myth: It takes ages to get pregnant after you stop taking the combined pill
Truth: Your fertility returns to normal soon after you stop taking the combined pill.

Myth: The hormones in the combined pill are harmful/dangerous
Truth: The combined pill contains estrogen and progestogen, which are similar to the hormones women produce naturally in their ovaries. There are some serious but rare risks involved with taking the combined pill but for most women the hormones are not harmful or dangerous.

How effective is the combined pill?

If the combined pill is taken according to instructions it is over 99 per cent effective. This means that less than one woman in 100 will get pregnant in a year. If the combined pill is **not** taken according to instructions, more women will become pregnant.

How does the combined pill work?

The main way the combined pill works is to stop ovulation each month. It also:

- Thickens the mucus from your cervix. This makes it difficult for sperm to move through it and reach an egg.
- Makes the endometrium thinner so it is less likely to accept a fertilised egg.

Where can I get the combined pill?

You can go to a contraception or sexual health clinic, or general practice.

If you prefer not to go to your own general practice, or if they don't provide contraceptive services, they can give you information about another practice or clinic. All treatment is free and confidential. You don't need to have a vaginal or breast examination or cervical screening test when you are first prescribed the combined pill.

Can anyone use the combined pill?

Not everyone can use the combined pill so your doctor or nurse will need to ask you about your own and your family's medical history. Do mention any illness or operations you have had. Some of the conditions which **may** mean you should not use the combined pill are:

- you think you might already be pregnant
- you smoke **and** are 35 years old or over
- you are 35 years old or over and stopped smoking less than a year ago
- you are very overweight
- you take certain medicines.

You have now or had in the past:

- thrombosis in any vein or artery
- a heart abnormality or circulatory disease, including hypertension
- very severe migraines or migraines with aura
- breast cancer or breast cancer within the last five years
- active disease of the liver or gall bladder
- diabetes with complications or diabetes for more than 20 years.

If you are healthy, don't smoke and there are no medical reasons for you not to take the combined pill, you can take it until your menopause. Women using the combined pill will need to change to another method of contraception at the age of 50 years.

What are the advantages of the combined pill?
- Doesn't interrupt sex.
- Usually makes your bleeds regular, lighter and less painful.
- May help with premenstrual symptoms.
- Reduces the risk of cancer of the ovary, uterus and colon..
- Reduces acne in some women
- May protect against pelvic inflammatory disease.
- May reduce the risk of fibroids, ovarian cysts and non-cancerous breast disease.

What are the disadvantages of the combined pill?
There are some serious side effects of the combined pill (see *Are there any risks?* below). In addition:
- you may get *temporary* side effects at first including headaches, nausea, breast tenderness and mood changes. If these do not stop within a few months, changing the type of combined pill may help
- the combined pill may increase your blood pressure
- the combined pill does not protect you against sexually transmitted infections, so you may need to use condoms as well
- breakthrough bleeding and spotting is common in the first few months of combined pill use (see *I'm bleeding on days I'm taking the combined pill, what should I do?* on page 100).

Are there any risks?
The combined pill can have some serious side effects, but these are not common. For most women the benefits of the combined pill outweigh the possible risks. All risks and benefits should be discussed with your doctor or nurse.
- A very small number of women may develop a venous thrombosis, an arterial thrombosis, heart attack or stroke. If you have ever had thrombosis, you should not use the combined pill. Some types of combined pill appear to be

associated with a slightly higher risk of venous thrombosis.

- The risk of venous thrombosis is greatest during the first year that you take the combined pill and if any of the following apply to you – you smoke, you are very overweight, are immobile for a long period of time or use a wheelchair, have severe varicose veins or a member of your immediate family had a venous thrombosis before they were 45 years old.
- The risk of arterial thrombosis is greatest if any of the following apply to you – you smoke, are diabetic, have hypertension, are very overweight, have migraines with aura, or a member of your immediate family had a heart attack or stroke before they were 45 years old.
- Research into the risk of breast cancer and hormonal contraception is complex and contradictory. Research suggests that users of all hormonal contraception appear to have a small increase in risk of being diagnosed with breast cancer compared to non-users of hormonal contraception. Further research is ongoing.
- Research suggests that there is a small increase in the risk of developing cervical cancer with longer use of estrogen and progestogen hormonal contraception.
- Some research suggests a link between using the combined pill and developing a very rare liver cancer.

See a doctor straightaway if you have any of the following:
- pain in the chest, including sharp pain which is worse when you breathe in
- breathlessness
- you cough up blood
- painful swelling in your leg(s)
- weakness, numbness, or bad 'pins and needles' in an arm or leg
- severe stomach pains
- a bad fainting attack or you collapse
- unusual headaches or migraines that are worse than usual
- sudden problems with your speech or eyesight
- jaundice.

If you go into hospital for an operation or you have an accident which affects the movement of your legs, tell the doctor that you are taking the combined pill. You may need to stop taking the combined pill or need other treatment to reduce the risk of developing thrombosis.

Are all combined pills the same?

No, there are three main types of combined pill and many different brands. They are taken differently.

- **Monophasic 21 day pills –** This is the most common type of combined pill. Each pill has the same amount of hormone in it. You take one a day for 21 days then no pills for the next seven days.
- **Phasic 21 day pills –** These pills contain different amounts of hormone so you must take them in the right order. There are two or three sections of different coloured pills in the pack. You take one pill a day for 21 days then no pills for the next seven days.
- **EveryDay (ED) pills –** There are 21 active pills containing hormones and seven inactive pills which don't contain any hormones (placebos). These look different to the active pills. You take one pill a day for 28 days with no break between packets. There are different types of EveryDay pills. Whichever type you take, you must take EveryDay pills in the right order.

Qlaira is a different type of combined pill and some of the instructions included here may not be relevant to it. Seek advice.

How do I start the first pack of combined pills?

These instructions apply to most types of combined pill. You can start the combined pill anytime in your menstrual cycle if you are not pregnant. If you start the combined pill on the first day of your period you will be protected from pregnancy immediately. You can also start the combined pill up to, and including, the fifth day of your period and you will be protected from pregnancy immediately.

However, if you have a short menstrual cycle with your period coming every 23 days or less, starting the combined pill as late as the fifth day of your cycle may not provide you with immediate contraceptive protection because you may ovulate early in your menstrual cycle. Talk to your doctor or nurse about this and whether you need to use additional contraception for the first seven days. If you start the combined pill at any other time in your menstrual cycle you will need to use additional contraception, such as condoms, for the first seven days of pill taking.

I've just had a baby. Can I use the combined pill?

You can start taking the combined pill three weeks (21 days) after you gave birth. Starting on day 21 you will be protected against pregnancy immediately. If you start later than day 21, use additional contraception for seven days.

If you are breastfeeding a baby under six months old, taking the combined pill may reduce your flow of milk. It is usually recommended that you use a different method of contraception.

Can I use the combined pill after a miscarriage or abortion?
You can start taking the combined pill immediately after a miscarriage or abortion. You will be protected from pregnancy immediately.

How do I take the combined pill?
21 day pills – Take your first pill from the bubble in the packet marked with the correct day of the week or the first pill of the first colour (phasic pills). Try to take it at the same time each day and take a pill every day until the pack is finished (21 days).

You then stop taking pills for seven days. During this week you may get a bleed. You don't have periods when you take a combined pill. What you have is a withdrawal bleed (which doesn't always happen). It is caused by you not taking hormones in the pill free week. Start your next pack on the eighth day (the same day of the week as you took your first pill). Do this whether or not you are still bleeding.

EveryDay pills – Take the first pill from the section of the packet marked 'start'. This will be an active pill. Take a pill every day until the pack is finished (28 days). You must take the pills in the correct order and try to take them at the same time each day. Taking the pills in the wrong order could mean that you are not protected against pregnancy.

During the seven days that you take the placebo pills you will get a withdrawal bleed. When you finish a pack you should start another pack the next day whether or not you are still bleeding.

EveryDay pills come with sticky strips of paper with the days of the week marked on them. These help you keep track of your pill taking. Instructions in the packet will tell you how to use them.

How important is it that I take the combined pill at the same time each day?
The combined pill is designed to be taken every day. It is very important that you take the pill each day as instructed. When taking your first pill, choose a convenient time for you. This can be any time of day. Taking a pill at the same time each day will help you to remember to take it regularly. **You have 'missed a**

pill' if you take it more than 24 hours later than your chosen time. If you do miss any pill(s) the important thing is not to stop taking it. Use the chart on page 99 to see what you should do if you've missed a pill.

Am I protected from pregnancy during the seven day break or the placebo week?
Yes. You are protected if:

- you have taken all the pills correctly **and**
- you start the next packet on time **and**
- nothing else has happened that might make the combined pill less effective (see the next question).

What should I do if I miss a pill or start my packet late?
Missing pills or starting the packet late may make the combined pill less effective. The chance of pregnancy after missing pills depends on:

- **when** pills are missed and
- **how many** pills are missed. Missing one pill anywhere in your pack or starting the new pack one day late is **not** a problem.

Depending on which type of combined pill you take, missing **more than one** or starting the packet **more than one** day late may affect your contraceptive cover. Use the chart on page 99 to see what you should do.

It is more risky to start a packet late and miss more than one pill. This is because during the seven day break or placebo week your ovaries are not getting any effects from the combined pill. If you make the break or placebo week longer you may ovulate. If you are not sure what to do, continue to take your pill, use additional contraception, such as condoms, and seek advice.

What should I do if I am sick or have diarrhoea?
If you vomit within **two** hours of taking a combined pill, it will not have been absorbed by your body. Take another pill as soon as you feel well enough. As long as you are not sick again your contraception will not be affected. Take your next pill at the normal time. If you continue to be sick, seek advice.

If you have very **severe** diarrhoea that continues for more than **24 hours**, this may make the combined pill less effective. Keep taking your pill at the normal time, but treat each day that you have severe diarrhoea as if you had missed a pill and follow the missed pill instructions in the chart on page 99.

How many pills have you missed?*

Up to two,
anywhere in the pack (only **one** if taking the pills Loestrin 20, Mercilon, Sunya or Femodette).

Take the last pill you missed now.

Continue taking the rest of the pack as usual.

No additional contraception needed.

You do not need to use emergency contraception.

Three or more,
(**two** if taking the pills Loestrin 20, Mercilon, Sunya or Femodette).

Take the last pill you missed now.

Continue taking the rest of the pack as usual.

Leave any earlier missed pills.

Use an extra method of contraception for the next seven days.

If you have had unprotected sex in the previous few days, you may need emergency contraception. Seek advice.

How many pills are left in the pack after the missed pill?

*If you miss pills and have also missed pills in your previous packet, speak to your doctor or nurse as you may need emergency contraception.

If you are taking the combined pill Qlaira and have missed a pill, the information on this chart may not apply to you. Seek advice.

Seven or more

Finish pack, have the usual seven day break or take the placebo tablets.

Less than seven

Finish pack and begin new one the next day. (This means missing out the break or not taking the placebo tablets.)

If I take other medicines will it affect my combined pill?

There are a few medicines that make the combined pill less effective. Ask your doctor, nurse or pharmacist for advice. Follow the instructions below if you are taking a medicine that affects the combined pill.

Common antibiotics – Continue taking your combined pill as usual and use an additional method of contraception, such as condoms, while taking the antibiotics and for seven days after you've finished them. If you get to the end of your packet or the end of the active pills in EveryDay pills while you are taking the antibiotics or still need to use additional contraception, then start a new packet straightaway. Do not have your usual seven day break or take your placebo tablets. You may or may not bleed, this is normal.

If you are given antibiotics in the first week of your pill packet and you have had sex recently you should seek advice as you may also need to use emergency contraception. If you are taking a common antibiotic for more than two weeks, you will need to follow different instructions. Your doctor or nurse can advise you.

Some other medicines – These include some medicines used to treat epilepsy, HIV and TB, and the complementary medicine St John's Wort. These types of drugs are called enzyme inducers. If you take these medicines talk to your doctor or nurse. It us often advised that you use a different method of contraception instead of the combined pill.

What if I want to change to a different type of combined pill?

It is easy to change from one combined pill to another. Talk to your doctor or nurse as you may need to miss out the break or placebo week or use additional contraception for a short time.

I'm bleeding on days when I'm taking the combined pill, what should I do?

Bleeding is very common when you first start taking the combined pill and is not usually anything to worry about. It may take up to three months to settle down. It is very important to keep taking the pills to the end of the packet, even if the bleeding is as heavy as your withdrawal bleed.

Bleeding may also be caused by you not taking the combined pill correctly or by a sexually transmitted infection. If it carries on or starts after you have used the combined pill for some time, seek advice.

I didn't bleed in my pill-free week – am I pregnant?

If you took all your pills correctly and you didn't have an upset stomach or take any other medicines which might have affected the combined pill, then it is very unlikely you are pregnant. So start your next packet at the right time. If you are worried ask your doctor or nurse for advice, or do a pregnancy test. Taking the combined pill does not affect a pregnancy test. Always take a test or speak to a health professional if you miss more than one bleed. If you do become pregnant, there is no evidence to show that taking the combined pill harms the baby.

Can I miss out a withdrawal bleed?

Yes. This is not harmful to do. If you are taking a monophasic pill (where all the pills are identical) you should start another packet straightaway and miss out the pill-free break. With EveryDay pills, miss out the placebo tablets. If you are taking a phasic pill, ask your doctor or nurse which pills to take. Sometimes you do still get some bleeding. This is nothing to worry about. If you have taken your pills correctly, you will still be protected against pregnancy.

What should I do if I want to stop taking the combined pill or try to get pregnant?

Ideally, it is easier to stop taking the combined pill at the end of the packet. If you don't want to wait until then seek advice because you can risk becoming pregnant if you have had sex recently. If you do not want to become pregnant use another method of contraception as soon as you stop taking the last active pill. Don't worry if your normal periods don't start immediately. For some women it can take a few months. If you want to try for a baby it is advisable to wait for one natural period before trying to get pregnant. This means the pregnancy can be dated more accurately and you can start pre-pregnancy care such as taking folic acid and stopping smoking. Ask your doctor or nurse for advice. Don't worry if you do get pregnant sooner, it will not harm the baby.

Should I give my body a break from the combined pill every few years or so?

No, you don't need to take a break because the hormones do not build up. There are no known benefits to your health or fertility from taking a break.

How often do I need to see a doctor or nurse?

When you first start the combined pill you will usually be given three months' supply to see how it suits you. After that you should go back to the doctor or nurse to get new supplies and to have your blood pressure checked. If there are no problems, you can be given up to one year's supply of the combined pill.

Chapter 12: The progestogen-only pill

This pill contains a progestogen hormone which is similar to the natural progesterone women produce in their ovaries. Progestogen-only pills are different to combined pills because they do not contain any estrogen. There are different types of progestogen-only pill available, some containing different progestogens.

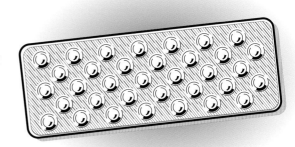

Myth busting

● **Myth: You have to take two pills a day if you are overweight**
● **Truth:** You only need to take one pill a day, regardless of how much you weigh.

● **Myth: The progestogen-only pill is a less effective/lower dose/safer version of the combined pill**
● **Truth:** The progestogen-only pill is not a different version of the combined pill – it is a different method of contraception. It only contains the hormone progestogen, whereas the combined pill contains estrogen and progestogen. They are as effective as each other and the different methods may suit different women.

● **Myth: It can only be used by older women or women who are breastfeeding**
● **Truth:** Most women can use the progestogen-only pill, not just those who are breastfeeding or are older.

Q A **How effective is the progestogen-only pill?**
If taken according to instructions the progestogen-only pill is over 99 per cent effective. This means that less than one woman in 100 will get pregnant in a year. If the progestogen-only pill is **not** taken according to instructions, more women will become pregnant.

How does the progestogen-only pill work?
The progestogen-only pill works in a number of ways:
- It mainly works by thickening the mucus from your cervix. This makes it difficult for sperm to move through it and reach an egg.
- It makes the endometrium thinner so it is less likely to accept a fertilised egg.
- It sometimes stops ovulation. This is the main action of one progestogen-only pill, Cerazette. This may mean that Cerazette is more effective than other progestogen-only pills, but research has not yet confirmed this.

Where can I get the progestogen-only pill?
You can go to a contraception or sexual health clinic or general practice. If you prefer not to go to your own general practice, or if they don't provide contraception services, they can give you information about another practice or clinic. All treatment is free and confidential. You don't need to have a vaginal or breast examination or cervical screening test when you are first prescribed the progestogen-only pill.

Can anyone use the progestogen-only pill?
Not everyone can use the progestogen-only pill and a doctor or nurse will ask you about your own and your family's medical history. Do mention any illness or operations you have had. Some of the conditions which **may** mean you should not use the progestogen-only pill are:
- you think you might already be pregnant
- you take certain medicines.

You have now or had in the past:
- heart disease or a stroke
- active disease of the liver
- current breast cancer or breast cancer within the last five years
- migraines with aura.

If you are healthy and there are no medical reasons for you not to take the progestogen-only pill, you can take it until your menopause or until you are 55 years old.

What are the advantages of the progestogen-only pill?
- It doesn't interfere with sex.
- You can use it if you are breastfeeding.
- It is useful if you cannot take estrogens, like those found in the combined pill, contraceptive patch and contraceptive vaginal ring.
- You can use it at any age, but it is especially useful if you smoke *and* are 35 or over.
- It may help with premenstrual symptoms and painful periods.

What are the disadvantages of the progestogen-only pill?
There are no serious side effects with the progestogen-only pill. However:
- You may not have regular periods while you are taking the progestogen-only pill. Your periods may be irregular, light, or more frequent or may stop altogether. This may settle down and is not harmful but you may find it annoying. If you have any concerns, see your doctor or nurse. Changing to a different progestogen-only pill may help.
- The progestogen-only pill does not protect you against sexually transmitted infections, so you may need to use condoms as well.
- You have to remember to take the pill at the same time every day.
- You may get some *temporary* side effects when you first start taking the progestogen-only pill, these should stop within a few months. They include spotty skin, breast tenderness, weight change and headaches.

Are there any risks?
The progestogen-only pill is a very safe pill to take but there are some risks.
- Some women may develop small fluid-filled cysts on their ovaries. These are not dangerous and do not usually need to be removed. Often there are no symptoms, but some women may have pelvic pain. These cysts usually disappear without treatment.
- Research about the risk of breast cancer, cervical cancer and hormonal contraception is complex and contradictory. Research suggests that users of all hormonal contraception appear to have a small increase in risk of being diagnosed with breast cancer compared to non-users of hormonal contraception. Further research is ongoing.

How do I start the progestogen-only pill?
You can start the progestogen-only pill anytime in your menstrual cycle if you are sure you are not pregnant. If you start the progestogen-only pill on the first day of your period you will be protected from pregnancy immediately. You can also start the progestogen-only pill up to and including the fifth day of your period and you will be protected from pregnancy immediately.

However, if you have a short menstrual cycle with your period coming every 23 days or less, starting the progestogen-only pill as late as the fifth day of your period may not provide you with immediate contraceptive protection. This is because you ovulate early in your menstrual cycle. You may wish to talk to your doctor or nurse about this and whether you need to use additional contraception for the first two days.

If you start the progestogen-only pill at any other time in your menstrual cycle use another contraceptive method for the first two days of your pill taking.

I've just had a baby. Can I take the progestogen-only pill?
The progestogen-only pill can be started any time after the birth. If you start the progestogen-only pill after day 21 you will need to use additional contraception for two days. You can breastfeed while you are taking the progestogen-only pill. A tiny amount of hormone enters your breast milk but research has shown this will not harm your baby.

Can I use the progestogen-only pill after a miscarriage or abortion?
You can start taking the progestogen-only pill immediately after a miscarriage or abortion. You will be protected from pregnancy immediately.

How do I take the progestogen-only pill?
When taking your first pill choose a convenient time to take it. This can be any time of the day. Once you have chosen a time you must then take one progestogen-only pill each day at this same time until you finish all the pills in the pack. You then start a new pack the next day so there are no breaks between packs.

What if I forget to take it on time?
For your pill to work it is important not to take it more than three hours (12 hours for Cerazette) after your chosen time. If you remember later than this, don't panic – see *What do I do if I miss a pill?* on page 107.

What if I want to change to a different pill?
If you are changing to another progestogen-only pill (or from the combined pill) you may be advised to start the new pill immediately or to start the day after you take your last pill. Do not have a break between packs. There is no need to wait for your period. You will then continue to be protected against pregnancy.

What should I do if I am sick or have diarrhoea?
If you vomit within **two** hours of taking the progestogen-only pill, it will not have been absorbed by your body. Take another pill as soon you feel well enough. As long as you are not sick again your contraception will not be affected. Take your next pill at the normal time. If you continue to be sick, seek advice.

If you have very **severe** diarrhoea that continues for more than **24 hours**, this may make the progestogen-only pill less effective. Keep taking your pill at the normal time, but treat each day that you have severe diarrhoea as if you had missed a pill and follow the missed pill instructions in the box on page 107.

If I take other medicines will it affect my progestogen-only pill?
If you are given a medicine by a doctor, nurse or hospital always say you are taking the progestogen-only pill. Commonly used antibiotics do not affect the progestogen-only pill. Medicines such as some of those used to treat epilepsy, HIV and TB and the complementary medicine St John's Wort may make it less effective. These types of drugs are called enzyme inducers. If you take these medicines, talk to your doctor or nurse about how to take the progestogen-only pill or whether you will need to use a different method of contraception.

What should I do if I think I'm pregnant?
If you took all your pills correctly and you didn't vomit, have severe diarrhoea or take any medicines which might affect the progestogen-only pill, then it is unlikely you are pregnant. Continue to take your pills as normal. There is no evidence that if you take the progestogen-only pill when you are pregnant it will harm the baby. If you are worried ask your doctor or nurse for advice or do a pregnancy test. Taking the progestogen-only pill does not affect a pregnancy test.

You should seek medical advice as soon as possible if you have a sudden or unusual pain in your lower abdomen or if your period is shorter or lighter than usual. These might be the warning signs of an ectopic pregnancy.

What do I do if I miss a pill?
If you are more than three hours* late

- Take a pill as soon as you remember. If you have missed more than one, only take one.
- Take your next pill at the usual time. This may mean taking two pills in one day. This is not harmful.
- You are **not** protected against pregnancy. Continue to take your pills as usual but use an additional method of contraception, such as condoms, for the next two days.

If you are less than three hours* late

- Take a pill as soon as you remember, and take the next one at the usual time. You are protected from pregnancy.

*12 hours if you are taking the progestogen-only pill, Cerazette.

I want to have a baby. Can I try to get pregnant as soon as I stop taking the progestogen-only pill?
You can try to get pregnant as soon as you stop taking the progestogen-only pill. You can stop taking the pill at any time. Ideally you should wait for one natural period before trying to get pregnant, so you will need to use another method of contraception, such as condoms. This means the pregnancy can be dated more accurately and you can start pre-pregnancy care such as taking folic acid and stopping smoking. You can ask your doctor or nurse for advice. Don't worry if you get pregnant sooner, it will not harm the baby.

How often do I need to see a doctor or nurse?
When you first start the progestogen-only pill you will usually be given three months' supply to see how it suits you. After that you should go back to the doctor or nurse to get new supplies and to have your blood pressure checked. If there are no problems, you can be given up to one year's supply of pills.

Chapter 13: Male condoms

Male condoms are a barrier method of contraception. They stop sperm meeting an egg. A male condom fits over a man's erect penis and stops sperm from entering the vagina. It is made of very thin latex (rubber) or polyurethane (plastic). Find out more about female condoms in Chapter 14.

Myth busting

- **Myth: You can use a male condom more than once**
- Truth: You must use a new male condom every time you have sex.

- **Myth: It's safer to use two male condoms at once**
- Truth: Using two male condoms together does not provide any additional contraceptive protection. In fact, the possible friction between the two means that they are more likely to tear or break.

- **Myth: The male condom will only fit average size men**
- Truth: Male condoms come in a range of shapes and sizes so that there is one to fit every penis.

How effective are male condoms?

If used according to instructions the male condom is 98 per cent effective. This means that two women in 100 will get pregnant in a year. If it is **not** used according to instructions more women will become pregnant.

Some novelty male condoms are designed purely for fun and should not be used for contraception. It will say so on the packet so check before you use them.

Can anything make male condoms less effective?

Sperm can get into the vagina during sex, even if you use a male condom. This may happen if:

- the penis touches the area around the vagina **before** a male condom is put on (pre-ejaculation fluid, which leaks out of the penis before ejaculation, may contain sperm)
- the condom splits
- you use the wrong type or size of condom
- you don't use a condom correctly
- you use too much or too little lubricant
- it slips off
- the condom gets damaged, for example by sharp fingernails or jewellery
- you use oil-based products (such as body lotions) with latex condoms. These damage the male condom.

If any of these happen, or if you have had sex without using contraception, you can get advice about emergency contraception (see Chapter 17: Emergency contraception).

Where can I get male condoms?

Male condoms are *free* from contraception and sexual health clinics and young people's services, and some general practices and genitourinary medicine (GUM) clinics. You can buy them from a pharmacy, by mail order or online as well as from vending machines, supermarkets, garages and other shops. They are available in different shapes and sizes.

What are the advantages of male condoms?

- You only need to use them when you have sex.
- They help to protect both partners from some sexually transmitted infections, including HIV.
- There are no serious side effects from using male condoms.
- They come in a variety of shapes and sizes to suit everyone.
- They are easily available.

What are the disadvantages of male condoms?
- Putting them on can interrupt sex.
- They can sometimes slip off or split.
- Some people are sensitive to latex condoms, though this is rare.
- A man has to pull out after he has ejaculated, and before the penis goes soft, holding the condom firmly in place.

Can anyone use male condoms?

Yes, male condoms are suitable for most people. Some men and women are sensitive to latex condoms. If this is a problem you can use male polyurethane condoms or female condoms.

Men who do not always keep their erection during sex may find it difficult to use a male condom.

When should I use lubricants with a condom?

Most male condoms come ready lubricated to make them easier to use. Some people also like to use additional lubrication. Any lubricant can be used with male polyurethane condoms.

However, if you are using a male latex condom you should never use oil-based products – such as body oils, creams, lotions or petroleum jelly – as a lubricant. This is because they can damage the latex and make the condom more likely to split.

Some ointments can also damage latex. If you are using medication in the genital area – for example, creams, pessaries, or suppositories – ask your doctor, nurse or pharmacist if it will affect latex condoms.

You can check the condom packaging to find out whether it is made from latex or polyurethane.

Some condoms don't have any lubricant on them so that you can choose not to use lubricant, or to use a lubricant of your own choice.

Q **Do I need to use spermicide?**

A No. If used correctly, male condoms are an effective method of contraception and you do not need additional spermicide.

Some male condoms are lubricated with spermicide, a chemical that kills sperm. These types of male condom are being phased out as research has shown that the spermicide commonly contains a chemical called Nonoxinol 9 which does not protect against sexually transmitted infections such as HIV and may even increase the risk of infection. If you can, avoid using spermicidally lubricated condoms and don't use additional spermicide as a lubricant.

Q **How soon can you use male condoms after having a baby?**

A You can use male condoms immediately after you have had a baby – using an additional lubricant can help to make sex more comfortable.

Q **Can male condoms be used after a miscarriage or abortion?**

A You can use male condoms immediately after having a miscarriage or abortion.

Q **The male condom or the female condom?**

A It's up to you and your partner to choose the condom which suits you best. You could try each of them before making up your mind. You may decide sometimes to use a male condom and other times a female condom.

Q **What condoms are best for oral sex?**

A Any condoms can be used for oral sex. However, flavoured condoms are a good option because they're not lubricated and come in a range of flavours to suit most people's tastes.

Q **What condoms are best for anal sex?**

A Standard condoms are suitable for anal sex – there is no evidence that stronger or thicker condoms are better or safer. It's very important that you use extra lubrication for anal sex to reduce the risk of the condom tearing.

Become a confident condom user! See Chapter 19.

How do I use a male condom?

You will find instructions on the condom packet or in a leaflet inside the pack. You can also ask your doctor, nurse or pharmacist.

- Use a new male condom each time you have sex.
- Check the 'use by' date on the packet. Be careful how you take the condom out of the packet – sharp fingernails and jewellery can tear it.
- Masturbate the penis a little before you put the condom on to provide some extra stimulation.
- Find the teat or closed end of the condom and squeeze it to get rid of air. This will also help you roll the condom on the right way round.

- Put the condom on when the penis is fully erect and **before** it touches the vagina or genital area. Still holding the end, roll the condom all the way down the penis. If it won't roll down then it's probably on inside out. If so, start again with a new condom as sperm could now be on the first one.
- You may find it easier and more comfortable to put the condom on if the foreskin is pulled back. This lets the foreskin move freely and reduces the risk of the condom tearing or slipping off.

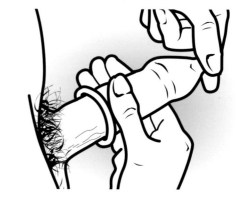

- As soon as the man has ejaculated, and before the penis goes soft, hold the condom firmly in place while pulling out. Do this slowly and carefully so you do not spill any semen.
- Take off the condom, wrap it and put it in a bin. Do not put it down the toilet.
- Make sure the penis does not touch the genital area again, and if you have sex again, use a new condom.

Can sperm travel through pores in the condom?

No. Neither latex nor polyurethane condoms have pores in the condom. When they are made they are also tested to make sure no holes have been created during the manufacturing process.

How are condoms tested to make sure they will work?

Condoms go through several different tests to check they are free from holes, the strength and stretch of the latex, the air pressure needed to burst one and the safety of the packaging.

Are there different types of condoms?

When choosing what condoms to use you are spoilt for choice. In addition to regular, average sized, latex and polyurethane condoms there are small ones and big ones, ribbed ones and studded ones, stimulating ones and dulling ones – a condom for every eventuality.

Regular condoms

Made from latex or polyurethane. They are an average length and width to suit most men and are straight sided with a round or teated end. Adult penis sizes do vary, but not by much. However, you may feel more comfortable with a larger or smaller condom.

Men come in all shapes and sizes ...

... and so do condoms

Larger condoms

These are condoms designed to fit a larger penis. They vary in size and some are a flared shape to improve comfort and make putting them on easier.

Smaller condoms

Often known as trim condoms, small condoms are designed for a thinner or shorter penis.

Ejaculation delayers

Most ejaculation delayer condoms contain benzocaine. Benzocaine is a low-strength local anaesthetic, similar to that used in throat lozenges and mouth ulcer treatments. It is put in the condom lubricant or teat and works by temporarily numbing the nerve endings of the penis.

Heightened stimulation condoms

Condoms for 'heightened stimulation' can make sex more pleasurable. Some contain a special lubricant that creates a warm or tingling sensation for both partners. Others contain extra lubricant to increase sensation. In addition to this, all brands now have at least one style of condom in their range that is textured – ribbed, dotted, studded – which is intended to increase sensation during sex.

Fun condoms

Coloured, flavoured, glow-in-the-dark and novelty condoms are all aimed to make sex more fun. If you have a novelty condom, check the packaging to make sure that it can be used to protect against pregnancy and sexually transmitted infections.

Strong condoms

These condoms are slightly thicker and sometimes have additional lubricant. They are usually made of latex. Strong condoms are not less likely to break.

"**Typical!** All I wanted was a big packet of THOSE NEW MANGO CONDOMS and they've sold out again."

Thin condoms

These condoms are thinner than a regular condom, providing greater sensitivity and a more natural feel for both partners.

Vegan condoms

In some condoms, the latex is free from animal products so they are suitable for vegans. Contact the Vegan Society to see which brands it recommends.

Where should I keep male condoms?

Always keep packets of condoms and individual condoms where they cannot be damaged by strong heat, sharp objects, light or damp.

Going on holiday?

Perhaps you are going away hoping to have sex, maybe you are travelling with a partner or maybe you've no intention of having sex while you are away. However you feel it's always a good idea to pack condoms – even if it's 'just in case'. If you are going abroad, take your favourite brand from the UK and take plenty! That way you can be sure you'll be safe and won't have to rely on a local brand which could be packaged in a foreign language or which may not have been produced to the same standards.

Chapter 14: Female condoms

Female condoms are a barrier method of contraception. They stop sperm meeting an egg. A female condom is made of very thin polyurethane (plastic). It is put in the vagina and loosely lines it. Find out more about male condoms in Chapter 13.

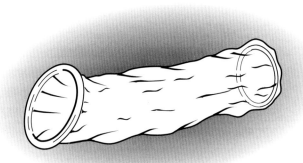

Myth busting

- **Myth: Using a female condom is like having sex in a crisp packet**
- **Truth:** Many men and women find they enjoy sex when using a female condom and it is nothing like having sex in a crisp packet.

- **Myth: A female condom can get lost inside you**
- **Truth:** The female condom is too big to fit through the cervix and therefore it can't get lost inside your body.

How effective are female condoms?
If used according to instructions the female condom is 95 per cent effective. This means that five women in 100 will get pregnant in a year. If it is *not* used according to instructions more women will become pregnant.

Can anything make female condoms less effective?
Sperm can get into the vagina during sex, even if you use a female condom. This may happen if:
- the penis touches the area around the vagina **before** a female condom is put in (pre-ejaculation fluid, which leaks out of the penis before ejaculation, may contain sperm)
- the condom gets pushed too far into the vagina
- the penis enters the vagina outside the condom by mistake

- the condom gets damaged, for example by sharp fingernails or jewellery
- the condom splits.

If any of these happen, or if you have had sex without using contraception, you can get advice about emergency contraception (see Chapter 17: Emergency contraception).

Where can I get female condoms?
Female condoms are *free* from contraception clinics and young people's services and some general practices and genitourinary medicine (GUM) clinics. You can also buy them from a pharmacy, online or by mail order. They are not as widely available as male condoms.

What are the advantages of female condoms?
- You only need to use them when you have sex.
- They help to protect both partners from some sexually transmitted infections, including HIV.
- There are no serious side effects from using female condoms.
- They can be inserted any time before sex.

What are the disadvantages of female condoms?
- Putting them on can interrupt sex.
- They can slip out or get pushed into the vagina.
- You need to make sure the penis is in the condom and not between the condom and the vagina, and that the open end of the condom stays outside the vagina.

Can anyone use female condoms?
Yes, female condoms are suitable for most people, although they may not be suitable for women who do not feel comfortable touching their genital area.

When should I use lubricants with a female condom?
Female condoms come ready lubricated to make them easier to use. Some people also like to use additional lubrication. Any lubricant can be used with female condoms as they are made of polyurethane. This includes body oils,

creams, lotions or petroleum jelly. If you are using medication in the genital area, for example, creams, suppositories or pessaries, you can still use female condoms.

I've just had a baby, can I use female condoms?
You can use female condoms immediately after you have had a baby – using an additional lubricant can help to make sex more comfortable.

Can I use female condoms after a miscarriage or abortion?
You can use female condoms immediately after having a miscarriage or abortion.

The male condom or the female condom?
It's up to you and your partner to choose the condom that suits you best. You could try each of them before making up your mind. You may decide sometimes to use a male condom and other times a female condom.

Do I need to use spermicide?
No. If used correctly, female condoms are an effective method of contraception and you do not need additional spermicide.

How do I use a female condom?
The packet contains an instruction leaflet.
- Use a new female condom every time you have sex. Check the 'use by' date on the packet.
- You can put the condom in any time **before** sex, but always before the penis touches the vagina or genital area. You can put the condom in when you are lying down, squatting or with one leg on a chair. Find the position that suits you best. Be careful how you take the condom out of the packet – sharp fingernails and jewellery can tear the condom.
- Hold the closed end of the condom and squeeze the inner ring between your thumb and

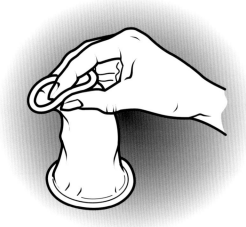

middle finger. Keeping your index finger on the inner ring helps you to insert the condom into the vagina.

- With your other hand, separate the labia. Put the squeezed ring into the vagina and push it up as far as you can.

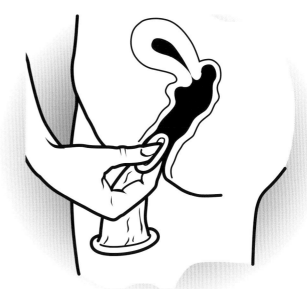

- Now put your index or middle finger, or both, inside the open end of the condom, until you can feel the inner ring. Push the inner ring as far back into the vagina as it will go. It will then be lying just above your pubic bone. (You can feel your pubic bone by inserting your index or middle finger into your vagina and curving it forward slightly.)

- Make sure that the outer ring lies close against the vulva.

- It is a good idea to guide the penis into the condom to make sure it does not enter the vagina outside the condom. Holding the outer ring in place, outside the vagina, also helps to stop the entire condom being accidentally pushed right into the vagina.

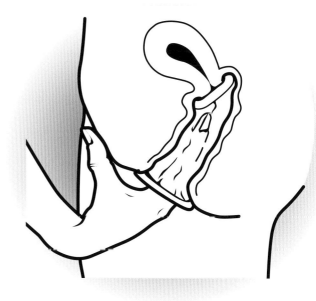

- As the female condom is loose-fitting, it will move during sex. But you will still be protected as long as the penis stays inside the condom.

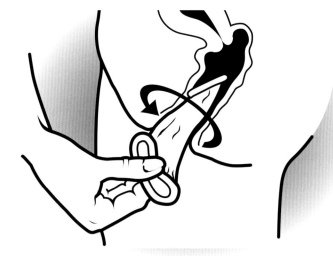

- To remove the condom, simply twist the outer ring to keep the semen inside. Then pull the condom out gently.
- Wrap the condom and put it in a bin. Do not put it down the toilet. Make sure the penis does not touch the genital area again, and if you have sex again, use a new condom.

 Where should I keep female condoms?
Always keep female condoms where they cannot be damaged by strong heat, sharp objects, light or damp.

> You can find lots of tips on using condoms in Chapter 19: Safer sex.

Chapter 15: The diaphragm or cap with spermicide

Diaphragms and caps are barrier methods of contraception. They fit inside your vagina and cover your cervix. They come in different shapes and sizes. Vaginal diaphragms are circular domes made of thin, soft latex (rubber) or silicone with a flexible rim. Cervical caps are smaller and are made of latex or silicone. To be effective, diaphragms and caps need to be used with a spermicide. Spermicides are chemicals that kill sperm.

Myth busting

Myth: You can leave a diaphragm or cap in all month
Truth: They should not be left in for more than the recommended time. This is 30–48 hours after sex, depending on the type you are using.

Myth: They should only be used by people who don't mind becoming pregnant
Truth: Diaphragms and caps are between 92–96 per cent effective when used with spermicide and according to instructions. Therefore, they are an effective method of contraception and can be used by many women.

How effective are diaphragms and caps?

If used according to instructions, diaphragms and caps are 92–96 per cent effective when used with spermicide. This means that between four and eight women in 100 will get pregnant in a year. If diaphragms and caps are **not** used according to instructions, more women will get pregnant.

How does a diaphragm or cap work?

A diaphragm or cap stops sperm reaching an egg. It covers your cervix while the spermicide kills any sperm. To be more effective in preventing a pregnancy, you must use spermicide with a diaphragm or cap (see *How do I put a diaphragm/cap in?* on pages 124–125).

Can anything make a diaphragm or cap less effective?

A diaphragm or cap will be less effective if:

- you don't use it every time you have sex
- it doesn't cover your cervix
- it isn't the right size
- you use it without spermicide
- you have sex three hours or more after you put it in and you don't use extra spermicide
- you don't use extra spermicide with your diaphragm or cap every time you have more sex
- you remove it too soon (less than six hours after the last time you had sex)
- you use oil-based products such as baby lotion, bath oils or some vaginal medicines (for example, pessaries) with latex diaphragms or caps. These can damage the latex.

If any of these happen, or if you have had sex without using contraception, you can get advice about emergency contraception (see Chapter 17: Emergency contraception).

> **What are the advantages of a diaphragm or cap?**
> - You only have to use it when you have sex.
> - It has no serious health risks.
> - You are in control of your contraception.
> - You can put it in at *any convenient time* before you have sex.

What are the disadvantages of a diaphragm or cap?

- Putting it in can interrupt sex.
- Some people find the spermicide messy.
- It can take time to learn how to use it.
- Cystitis can be a problem for some women who use a diaphragm. Ask the doctor or nurse to check the size of your diaphragm if you get cystitis. Changing to a slightly smaller or softer-rimmed (coil spring) diaphragm or to a cap may help.
- Some people are sensitive to the chemicals in latex or spermicide. This may cause irritation in some women or a partner.

Can anyone use a diaphragm or cap?

Most women can use a diaphragm or cap. A diaphragm or cap may not be suitable if you:

- have vaginal muscles which can't hold a diaphragm
- have a cervix which is an unusual shape, in an awkward position or if you cannot reach it
- are sensitive to the chemicals in latex or spermicide
- have repeated urinary infections
- have a vaginal infection (wait until after the infection has cleared)
- have ever had toxic shock syndrome
- do not feel comfortable touching your vagina.

If you have a high risk of getting a sexually transmitted infection, for example if you or a partner has more than one partner, it may be advisable not to use a diaphragm or cap. Research shows that spermicide which contains Nonoxinol 9, does not protect against sexually transmitted infections. It may even increase the risk of getting a sexually transmitted infection such as chlamydia or HIV.

I've just had a baby. Can I use a diaphragm or cap?

You may need a different size diaphragm or cap after you have had a baby. It is advisable to wait until at least six weeks after having a baby before using a diaphragm or cap.

Can I use a diaphragm or cap after an abortion?

Yes you can, although you may need a different size diaphragm or cap after a miscarriage or abortion.

Where can I get a diaphragm or cap?

You can get a diaphragm or cap from contraception clinics and young people's services, and some general practices and genitourinary medicine (GUM) clinics. If you know the size and type of diaphragm or cap you use, you can buy them from a pharmacy.

How do I put a diaphragm in?

Diaphragms come with instructions and a doctor or nurse will show you how to put it in. The different types of diaphragm are all used in a similar way.

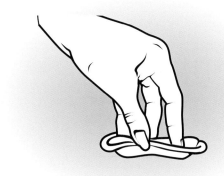

- With clean hands put a small amount of spermicide on each side of the diaphragm (approximately two 2cm strips). Some women find that putting a little spermicide on some of the rim makes the diaphragm easier to put in.
- Put your index finger on top of the diaphragm and squeeze it between your thumb and other fingers.
- Slide the diaphragm into your vagina upwards and backwards. This should ensure that the diaphragm covers your cervix.

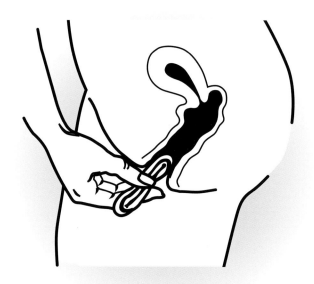

- Always check that your cervix is covered. It feels like the end of your nose.
- If your cervix is not covered, take the diaphragm out by hooking your finger under the rim or loop (if there is one) and pulling downwards and try again.
- Some women squat while they put their diaphragm in. Others lie down or stand with one foot up on a chair. You will need to find out which position is easiest for you.

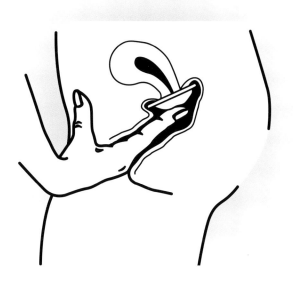

How do I put a cap in?

Caps come with instructions. The different types of cap are all used in a similar way.
- Fill one-third of the cap with spermicide but don't put any spermicide around the rim as this will stop the cap from staying in place. The silicone cap has a groove between the dome and the rim; some spermicide should also be placed there.
- Squeeze the sides of the cap together and hold it between your thumb and first two fingers. The cap must fit neatly over your cervix. It stays in place by suction.
- Always check that your cervix is covered. Depending on the type of cap, you may need to add extra spermicide after it has been put in.

How do I take out my diaphragm or cap?

You must leave all types of diaphragm and cap in place for **at least six hours** after the last time you had sex. You can leave it for longer, but don't leave a diaphragm or cap in for more than the recommended time. For latex types this is 30 hours, including the minimum six hours and for the silicone cap, 48 hours including the minimum six. Take it out by gently hooking your finger under the rim, loop or strap and pulling downwards.

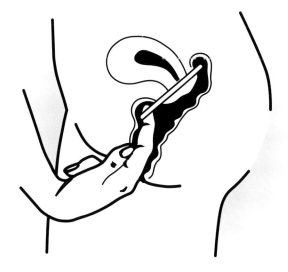

How do I look after my diaphragm or cap?

When you take your diaphragm or cap out, wash it in warm water with a mild, unperfumed soap. Then rinse it thoroughly. Dry it carefully and keep it in its container in a cool, dry place. Never boil your diaphragm or cap, never use disinfectant or detergent to clean it or use talcum powder with it. Do not use any oil-based product with latex types as it will damage them.

Before use, check your diaphragm or cap for tears or holes by holding it up to the light and having a good look at it. Be careful with your fingernails and jewellery. If your diaphragm goes out of shape, squeeze it gently back to its circular shape. Your diaphragm or cap may become discoloured. But don't worry, this will not make it less effective.

Can I use my diaphragm or cap during my period?

It is not recommended that use a diaphragm or cap during your period because of a possible risk of toxic shock syndrome.

Can I have a bath when I've got my diaphragm or cap in?

Put your diaphragm or cap in after a bath rather than before. Water may dislodge it or wash away the spermicide. Have a shower rather than a bath during the six hours after you have had sex when you need to keep your diaphragm or cap in.

The effect of swimming or water sports has not been studied, but it is likely to be small.

What is a practice diaphragm or cap?

A doctor or nurse will sometimes fit you with a practice diaphragm or cap that should be the right size for you. Practice diaphragms and caps give you time and privacy to find out if the method is suitable for you and to learn how to use it properly. While you are learning to use it, don't rely on it to stop you getting pregnant. You will need to use an additional method of contraception if you have sex.

During this time put the diaphragm or cap in and check that it covers your cervix. Have sex with the diaphragm or cap in place and leave it in for a few hours to find out if it is comfortable for you and a partner. It is also a good idea to use the spermicide jelly or cream to see how this feels.

When you go back to get it checked, wear the diaphragm or cap so the doctor or nurse can check that you have put it in properly and that it is the right size.

How often do I need to see a doctor or nurse?

Once you have a diaphragm or cap that you are happy with you only need to see a doctor or nurse to replace it or if you have any questions or concerns. You may need a different size diaphragm or cap if you gain or lose more than 3kg (7lbs) in weight.

Chapter 16: Natural family planning

This chapter gives you information on how natural family planning can help you to avoid pregnancy. Fertility awareness involves being able to identify the signs and symptoms of fertility during the menstrual cycle so you can plan or avoid pregnancy.

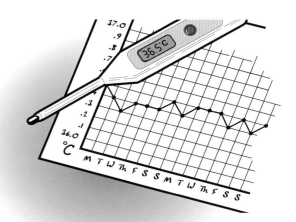

Myth busting

- **Myth: The 'safe period' means that you can only have sex during your period**
- **Truth:** You can have sex at anytime in your cycle when you are not fertile. You can also have sex during your fertile time as long as you use an additional barrier method of contraception such as condoms.

- **Myth: You can't use natural family planning if you don't have a regular partner**
- **Truth:** Natural family planning allows you to determine *your* fertile time and to avoid sex when you are fertile. It does not matter whether the person you have sex with is a regular partner or not, it only matters if you are fertile at the time or not.

What is the menstrual cycle?
The menstrual cycle is the time from the first day of your period to the day before your next period starts. The average length of the menstrual cycle is around 28 days, although many women have longer or shorter cycles and this is normal. Regardless of how long or short the cycle is, ovulation will usually happen around 10–16 days *before* the start of the next period. During your menstrual cycle:

- Eggs develop in your ovaries and usually one is released.

- The mucus in the cervix changes to allow sperm to pass more easily through the cervix to reach the egg.
- The endometrium thickens to prepare for a possible pregnancy.
- If the egg is not fertilized by sperm and you don't get pregnant the endometrium is shed as your period, which signals the beginning of a new menstrual cycle.

The menstrual cycle is controlled by your body's natural hormones – estrogen and progesterone. More information on the menstrual cycle is provided in Chapter 1: You and your body.

How does natural family planning work?
Natural family planning works by observing and recording your body's different natural signs or fertility indicators on each day of your menstrual cycle. The main fertility indicators are:
- recording your body temperature
- monitoring cervical secretions (cervical mucus)
- calculating how long your menstrual cycle lasts.

Changes in these fertility indicators can help you to identify your fertile time. You can also use fertility monitoring devices (see *How do I use fertility monitoring devices?* on page 134).

How long does the fertile time last?
The fertile time lasts for around 8–9 days of each menstrual cycle. This is because the egg lives for up to 24 hours. Occasionally, more than one egg is released during ovulation (within 24 hours of the first egg being released) and sperm can live inside a woman's body for up to seven days. This means that if you have sex as much as seven days before ovulation you may still get pregnant.

How effective is natural family planning?
If used according to teaching and instructions, natural family planning methods are up to 99 per cent effective, depending on which method is used. This means that up to one woman in 100 will get pregnant in a year. If natural family planning methods are **not** used according to instructions, more women will get pregnant.

Natural family planning is more effective when taught by a specialist natural family planning teacher, and when more than one fertility indicator is used. Some people choose to combine their fertility awareness knowledge with male or female condoms – this is sometimes known as fertility awareness combined methods. The effectiveness of this depends on how well you use male or female condoms.

What are the advantages of natural family planning?
- Using fertility awareness makes you more aware of your fertility and can help to plan a pregnancy or to avoid a pregnancy.
- It does not involve using any chemicals or physical products.
- There are no physical side effects.
- It can help you recognise normal and abnormal vaginal secretions.
- It can help you to communicate about your fertility and sexuality.
- It is acceptable to all faiths and cultures.

What are the disadvantages of natural family planning?
- It takes 3–6 menstrual cycles to learn effectively.
- You have to keep daily records.
- Some events, such as illness, lifestyle, stress or travel, may make fertility indicators harder to interpret.
- You need to avoid sex or use male or female condoms during the fertile time.
- Natural methods don't protect you against sexually transmitted infections.

Can anyone use natural family planning?
Most women can use natural methods as long as they receive good instructions and support. They can be used at all stages of your reproductive life, whatever age you are. Natural family planning may not be a suitable method for some women who do not have periods.

It may take longer to recognise your fertility indicators and to start to use natural family planning if you have irregular cycles, or at certain times, for example after stopping hormonal contraception, after having a baby, during breastfeeding, after an abortion or miscarriage, or when approaching the menopause.

How do I record the fertility indicators?
Some natural methods rely on using only one of the fertility indicators. Other methods use two or more indicators, which is more effective.

How do I record the temperature fertility indicator?
The hormones estrogen and progesterone cause your body temperature to change throughout the menstrual cycle – it rises slightly after you have ovulated. You can chart these changes by recording your temperature each day to show you when the fertile time ends. Fertility charts are available from Fertility UK (see sample on page 132 and Chapter 22: Useful organisations). You should use a special mercury fertility thermometer or digital thermometer which will show the small changes in temperature more easily. Ear or forehead thermometers are not accurate enough to use for natural family planning.

Do I need to take my temperature at a particular time?
You need to take your temperature before you get out of bed or after you have had at least three hours rest. This is known as your basal body temperature (BBT) or waking temperature. This should be done at the same time each day and before you have anything to eat or drink.

The fertile time ends when you have recorded temperatures for three days in a row, which are higher than **all** the previous six days. The difference in temperature will be about 0.2 degrees Centigrade (0.4 degrees Farenheit).

Can anything alter the temperature readings?
Certain activities or events can alter your temperature readings and can make them less accurate. For example, if you:
- take your temperature earlier or later than normal
- use poor equipment or record findings badly
- have an illness, such as cold or flu, drink alcohol or oversleep (this can make your temperature go up)
- are taking pain relieving drugs, including aspirin (this can make your temperature go down).

The temperature indicator on its own does not help you to find the start of your fertile time.

Month and year		March							
Date		8	9	10	11	12	13	14	15
Day		W	T	F	S	S	M	T	W

Notes and comments	°C 37.1								
	37.0								
	36.9								
	36.8				●	●			
	36.7	●							
	36.6		●				●		
	36.5			●					●
	36.4							●	
	36.3								
Sexual intercourse	Circle day of cycle	1	2	3	4	5	6	7	8
Cervical Secretions	Wet, slippery, clear, stretchy								
	Moist, white, cloudy, sticky								
	Dry. No secretions seen or felt						▓	▓	▓
	Period	▓	▓	▓	▓	▓			
Cervix	High, soft, open								
	Low, firm, closed						●	●	●
Fertility devices	Use of test sticks								

How do I monitor the cervical secretions fertility indicator?

The amount of estrogen and progesterone varies in the menstrual cycle and this alters the quantity and type of cervical mucus. By monitoring the changes in your cervical secretions you can learn to identify the start and end of your fertile time.

- After your period you may notice a few days when your vagina and vulva feels dry and you can't see or feel any cervical secretions.
- As the level of estrogen rises, your body prepares for ovulation, the secretions produced by the cervix begin to change in texture and increase in amount and sensation. At first, they feel moist, sticky and appear white or creamy in

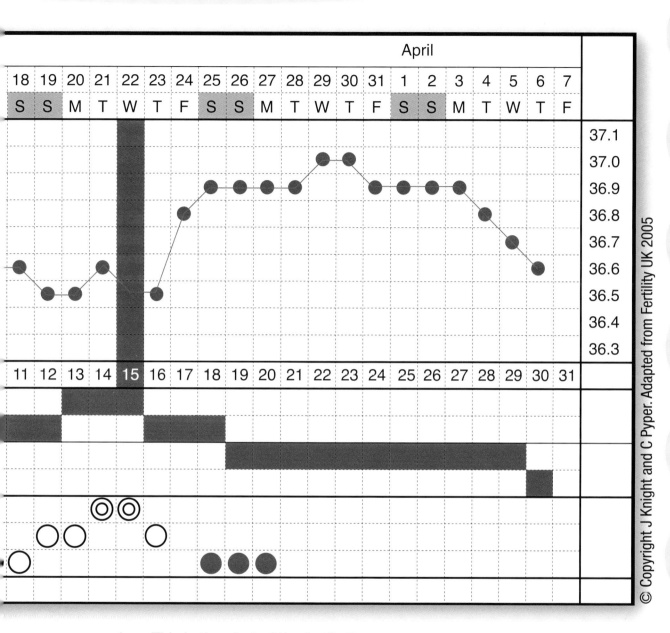

													April							
18	19	20	21	22	23	24	25	26	27	28	29	30	31	1	2	3	4	5	6	7
S	S	M	T	W	T	F	S	S	M	T	W	T	F	S	S	M	T	W	T	F

colour. This is the start of the fertile time.

- Just before ovulation the secretions become clearer, wetter, stretchy and slippery like raw egg white. This is known as fertile mucus and is a sign that you are at your most fertile.
- After ovulation the cervical secretions return to being thicker and sticky and after three days you will no longer be fertile.

The amount and quality of cervical secretions will vary from woman to woman and also from one cycle to the next.

© Copyright J Knight and C Pyper. Adapted from Fertility UK 2005

Can I combine temperature and cervical secretions fertility indicators?
Yes. Combining the temperature and cervical secretions indicators acts as a double check and increases the effectiveness of natural family planning. The fertile time starts at the first sign of **any** cervical secretions and ends after the third high temperature has been recorded and all three high temperatures occur after the last day of having wet or clear, slippery secretions (the peak day).

How can I work out how long my menstrual cycle lasts?
The length of your cycles can help you to work out the start of your fertile time. Keep a record of the length of your last six cycles, then find your shortest cycle and subtract 20 days to find the first fertile day. However, calculating your cycle length is not a reliable way of working out the end of your fertile time and this should **not** be used on its own as a fertility indicator.

How do I monitor changes to my cervix?
During your menstrual cycle your cervix changes in position and feels different. Around your fertile time the cervix will feel higher in the vagina, soft and slightly open. During your infertile time your cervix will feel low in the vagina, firm to touch and closed. These changes are not reliable enough to be used on their own as a fertility indicator.

Are there any other fertility indicators?
Some women may be aware of pain around ovulation or changes in their breasts, skin, mood or sex drive. These are the least reliable indicators of your fertile time.

How do I use fertility monitoring devices?
You can buy a number of different fertility devices at pharmacies. They work by monitoring changes in temperature, urine or saliva. In the UK the main product available is Persona. This consists of a small handheld computerised monitor and a series of urine test sticks which measure hormonal changes. Persona interprets these changes and can predict the fertile and infertile times of your menstrual cycle. If you use Persona according to the instructions, it is around 94 per cent effective. This means that at least six women in 100 will get pregnant in a year.

Computerised thermometers work by combining information about the length of your menstrual cycle and temperature. More research is needed about the effectiveness of these products.

Luteinising hormone (LH) dipstick tests or ovulation predictor kits are designed to be used by women planning a pregnancy. They are not effective as a natural family planning method.

Can I use breastfeeding as a natural family planning method?
You can find out more about using breastfeeding as a contraceptive method in Chapter 18: Using contraception after you've had a baby.

If I have to use hormonal emergency contraception will it affect my fertility indicators?
Yes. Using hormonal emergency contraception will upset your normal hormone pattern and alter your fertility indicators. After using hormonal emergency contraception you should not rely on your natural family planning indicators for two complete menstrual cycles. This allows time for your cycle to return to normal and for your natural family planning indicators to be reliable.

Are there any other natural family planning methods?
Two other natural family planning methods are being researched. These are called The Standard Days Method and The TwoDay Method. These are not in general use in the UK.

Where can I get help with natural family planning?
If you decide to use natural family planning you need to find someone to teach you how to use it. General practice and contraception clinics do not often teach natural family planning so you may need to find your own teacher. Some teachers charge a fee. Contact Fertility UK or the FPA helpline for help finding a natural family planning teacher (see Chapter 22: Useful Organisations).

Chapter 17: Emergency contraception

If you have had unprotected sex, that is, sex without using contraception, or think your contraception might have failed, you can use emergency contraception. There are two methods of emergency contraception:

- hormonal emergency contraception (known as the emergency contraceptive pill), and
- the emergency intrauterine device (IUD). The IUD is the most effective.

If you act quickly, emergency contraception will usually prevent pregnancy.

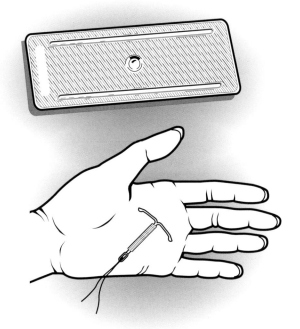

Myth busting

- **Myth: Emergency contraception can only be used once**
- **Truth:** There is no limit to the amount of times you can use emergency contraception. However, the other contraceptives in this book are more effective in preventing unplanned pregnancy.

- **Myth: If the emergency contraceptive pill fails, the baby will be harmed**
- **Truth:** The emergency pill has not been shown to affect a pregnancy or harm a developing baby.

- **Myth: Hormonal emergency contraception uses huge doses of hormones**
- **Truth:** Hormonal emergency contraception contains a higher dose of hormone than the daily combined or progestogen-only pill – this is to disrupt your menstrual cycle. However, the dose is safe.

- **Myth: Only irresponsible women use emergency contraception**
- **Truth:** Women from all walks of life may need emergency contraception for many different reasons.

Does emergency contraception cause an abortion?

No. Emergency contraception may stop ovulation, stop the fertilisation of an egg, or stop a fertilised egg from implanting in the uterus. Medical research and legal judgement are quite clear that emergency contraception (the pill or an IUD) prevents pregnancy and is not abortion.

Abortion can only take place after a fertilised egg has implanted in the uterus. People who believe life begins when the egg is fertilised may not wish to use the emergency contraception methods outlined in this chapter.

Where can I get emergency contraception?

You can get the emergency contraceptive pill and the emergency IUD **free** from:
- a contraception clinic
- any general practice that provides contraceptive services
- any young person's service or Brook clinic
- any sexual health clinic
- some genitourinary medicine (GUM) clinics.

You can also get the emergency contraceptive pill **free** from:
- most NHS walk-in centres (in England only)
- some pharmacies (there may be age restrictions)
- most NHS minor injuries units
- some hospital accident and emergency departments (phone first to check).

You can **buy** the emergency contraceptive pill from:
- most pharmacies if you are 16 years old or over
- some fee-paying clinics.

The price will vary but at the pharmacy it will cost around £25. All the advice and treatment you receive is confidential – wherever you receive it.

Method 1: The emergency contraceptive pill

What is the emergency contraceptive pill?

The emergency contraceptive pill is a tablet containing progestogen, a hormone which is similar to the natural progesterone women produce in their ovaries.

How do I take it?

You will be given one pill to take. It should be taken within three days (72 hours) of having unprotected sex. **It is more effective the sooner it is taken**.

How does the emergency contraceptive pill work?

The emergency contraceptive pill is most likely to stop or delay ovulation. It may also stop a fertilised egg implanting in your uterus.

How effective is the emergency contraceptive pill?

It is very effective and is more effective the sooner it is taken after sex. However, it is not as effective as using other methods of contraception regularly and does not protect you against sexually transmitted infections.

Of the pregnancies that could be expected to have occurred if no emergency contraception had been used, the emergency contraceptive pill will prevent:

- up to 95 per cent if taken within 24 hours
- up to 85 per cent if taken between 25–48 hours
- up to 58 per cent if taken between 49–72 hours.

The emergency contraceptive pill may be considered for use up to 120 hours after unprotected sex but it is not known how effective it will be. An emergency IUD is more effective at this stage (see *Method 2: The emergency IUD* on page 142). Get advice from your doctor, nurse or pharmacist.

Who can use the emergency contraceptive pill?

Most women can use the emergency contraceptive pill. This includes women who are breastfeeding and women who can't use estrogens – the hormone that is used in the combined pill, the contraceptive vaginal ring and the contraceptive patch. However, if you are taking certain prescribed medicines, or complementary medicines such as St John's Wort, you will need special advice and the dose of the emergency contraceptive pill may need to be increased. The emergency IUD may be a preferred option as there are no medicines known to affect it.

I've just had a baby. Can I use the emergency contraceptive pill?

Contraception needs to be used from day 21 after the birth of a baby. If you have sex before this time you will not get pregnant. Emergency contraception can be used safely after day 21 even by women who are breastfeeding.

Can I use the emergency contraceptive pill after a miscarriage or abortion?

Yes, you can use the emergency contraceptive pill immediately as you can become pregnant again very quickly following a miscarriage or abortion.

What are the side effects?

- There are no serious short- or long-term side effects from using the emergency contraceptive pill.
- Some women may feel sick, dizzy or tired, or may get headaches, breast tenderness or abdominal pain.
- A very small number of women will vomit.
- It can disrupt your periods (see the following question).

How will the emergency contraceptive pill affect my next period?

- Your next period is likely to either come on time or be a few days early or late. For some women it can be up to a week late or sometimes even later.
- You may have some irregular bleeding between taking the emergency contraceptive pill and your next period. This can range from spotting to being quite heavy.

Do I need to see a doctor or nurse after I've taken the emergency contraceptive pill?

Not usually, but do go and see a doctor or nurse if:

- you think you might be pregnant
- your next period is more than seven days late
- your period is shorter or lighter than usual
- you have any sudden or unusual pain in your lower abdomen.

These could be signs of an ectopic pregnancy – a pregnancy that occurs outside the uterus, usually in a fallopian tube. Although this is not common, it is very serious.

You should see a doctor or nurse if:

- you want to talk about using regular contraception

- you want advice about using or changing your current method of contraception
- you are worried that you might have caught a sexually transmitted infection.

Can the emergency contraceptive pill fail?
The emergency contraceptive pill is very effective and should be taken as soon as possible after unprotected sex. However, in some women it fails and they become pregnant even though the pill was taken correctly.

You may also become pregnant if you:
- delay taking the emergency contraceptive pill
- vomit within taking two hours of taking the pill
- have unprotected sex at another time, either since your last period or since taking the emergency contraceptive pill.

What if I vomit within two hours of taking the emergency contraceptive pill?
Speak to your doctor, nurse or pharmacist. They may give you another pill and a medicine to stop you vomiting again, or suggest having an emergency IUD fitted (see *Method 2: The emergency IUD* on page 142). If you vomit later than two hours, don't worry, the pill will have been absorbed.

How will I know if the emergency pill has worked?
If you have taken the pill correctly and your next period seems normal, it is unlikely that you will be pregnant. After you have taken the emergency contraceptive pill it is recommended that you do a pregnancy test to make sure you are not pregnant if:
- you think you feel pregnant
- you have not had a normal period within three weeks of taking the emergency contraceptive pill
- you do not have a bleed when you have the seven day break from using the contraceptive patch, combined pill or the contraceptive vaginal ring, or when you take the placebo tablets with EveryDay combined pills.

A pregnancy test result will be accurate if the test is done from three weeks after the last time you had unprotected sex. It will not be affected if you are taking regular hormonal contraception.

Are there any risks if the emergency contraceptive pill fails?

The emergency contraceptive pill has not been shown to affect a pregnancy or harm a developing baby. As with any pregnancy there is a small chance that an ectopic pregnancy may occur. If you think that you might be pregnant it is important to seek advice as soon as possible.

Will the emergency contraceptive pill protect me from pregnancy until my next period?

No. The emergency contraceptive pill will not protect you from pregnancy if you have unprotected sex again. Seek advice – you can use emergency contraception again.

Can I continue to use regular contraceptive pills, the contraceptive patch or the contraceptive vaginal ring after the emergency contraceptive pill?

Yes. If you needed emergency contraception because you forgot some of your regular pills or did not use the patch or the vaginal ring correctly, you should take a contraceptive pill again, apply a new patch or insert a new vaginal ring within 12 hours of taking the emergency contraceptive pill. You will need an additional contraceptive, such as condoms, for:

- seven days with the patch, the vaginal ring, and the combined pill
- two days with the progestogen-only pill.

How many times can I use the emergency contraceptive pill?

You can take the emergency contraceptive pill as many times as you need to and more than once in any menstrual cycle. It is not dangerous to do this but it may disrupt your periods. However, using the emergency contraceptive pill is **not** as effective as using other methods of contraception.

Can someone else get the emergency contraceptive pill for me?

You need to get the emergency contraceptive pill from the doctor, nurse or pharmacist yourself. Someone else will only be given it on your behalf in exceptional circumstances.

How can I buy the emergency contraceptive pill from a pharmacist?

If you are 16 or over, you can ask the pharmacist for the emergency contraceptive pill. They will need to ask you some questions as there are some circumstances when they may not be able to sell it to you, for example if:

- it has been more than 72 hours since you had unprotected sex
- you have had unprotected sex more than once in the menstrual cycle
- you think that you might already be pregnant
- you are taking certain prescribed or complementary medicines
- you have certain health conditions.

In these circumstances you will need to see a doctor or nurse.

Can I get emergency contraceptive pills in advance?
Yes, if you are worried about your contraceptive method failing, you are going on holiday, or you cannot get emergency contraception easily. Ask your doctor or nurse about this.

Method 2: The emergency IUD

What is the emergency IUD?
An emergency IUD is the same as the IUD, but it is fitted in an emergency situation. You can find out more in Chapter 6: The intrauterine device (IUD). It is a small plastic and copper device that is put into your uterus by a trained doctor or nurse. It can be fitted up to five days after unprotected sex at any time in the menstrual cycle provided this is the **only** unprotected sex that has occurred since your last period.

If you have had unprotected sex more than once since your last period then an emergency IUD can be fitted up to five days after the earliest time you would have ovulated.

If the emergency IUD cannot be fitted immediately you may be advised to take the emergency contraceptive pill in the meantime.

How does an emergency IUD work?
It may stop an egg being fertilised or implanting in your uterus.

How effective is an emergency IUD?
The emergency IUD is the most effective method of emergency contraception. It will prevent up to 99 per cent of pregnancies expected to occur if no emergency contraception had been used.

Who can use an emergency IUD?

Most women can use an emergency IUD for emergency contraception.
An emergency IUD may be suitable if:
- you want to use the most effective method of emergency contraception
- you do not want to, or cannot take progestogen
- you want to use the IUD as an ongoing method of contraception.

I've just had a baby. Can I use the emergency IUD?

Contraception needs to be used from day 21 after the birth of a baby, if
you have sex before this you will not get pregnant. However, an emergency
IUD is not normally recommended before 28 days after the birth. If you
need to, you can use the emergency contraceptive pill until this time.

Can I use the emergency IUD after a miscarriage or abortion?

Women can become pregnant again very quickly following a miscarriage
or abortion. It will depend how pregnant you were before the abortion or
miscarriage as to whether it would be advisable to use an emergency IUD
– a health professional can help you decide which method of emergency
contraception to use.

What are the disadvantages of using an IUD for emergency contraception?

- It is not as easily available as the emergency contraceptive pill.
- Not all women can use the emergency IUD, for example, women who
  have certain problems with their cervix or uterus.
- There is a very small chance of getting an infection in your uterus within
  the first 20 days after an emergency IUD is put in. If you have been at risk
  of getting a sexually transmitted infection you may have screening tests
  done at the time the emergency IUD is fitted and you may be given some
  antibiotics. This will help reduce the chance of getting a pelvic infection.
- An emergency IUD might go through (perforate) your uterus or cervix
  when it is fitted. This may cause pain but often there are no symptoms.
  If this happens, the emergency IUD may need to be removed by surgery.
  Perforation is uncommon when the emergency IUD is fitted by an
  experienced doctor or nurse.
- The emergency IUD can be pushed out by your uterus (expulsion) or
  it can move (displacement). This is not common.

How is the emergency IUD put in?

Find out more in Chapter 6: The intrauterine device (IUD).

How will I know that the emergency IUD is still in place?

Find out more about how to check the emergency IUD is still in place in Chapter 6: The intrauterine device (IUD).

When will I get my next period?

Your next period should come at about the same time as you would normally expect it. If you have not had a normal period within three weeks of having the emergency IUD fitted it's recommended that you do a pregnancy test.

Are there any risks if the emergency IUD fails?

The emergency IUD is highly effective. However, if it does fail and you become pregnant, there is a risk that the emergency IUD can cause a miscarriage or that an ectopic pregnancy may occur. If you know that you are pregnant, or think that you might be, it is important to seek advice as soon as possible.

Do I need to see a doctor or nurse after the emergency IUD is fitted?

Yes. It is recommended that you see a doctor or nurse 3–4 weeks after the emergency IUD is fitted, whether or not you have had a period. This is to:

- check you are not pregnant (if you have not had a normal period)
- discuss any problems
- remove the emergency IUD if this is what you want
- discuss your future contraceptive needs.

If you are worried about your emergency IUD contact your doctor or nurse as soon as you can. You should see your doctor or nurse immediately if you think you are pregnant or have any of the following:

- a sudden or unusual pain in your lower abdomen
- a shorter, lighter or delayed period
- an unusual or smelly discharge from the vagina
- a high temperature.

These could be signs of an ectopic pregnancy or an infection which can be serious.

Will the emergency IUD protect me from pregnancy until my next period?
Yes. As soon as it's fitted it will provide ongoing contraception until it is taken out. If you want to, you can carry on using this method as your regular contraception. You can discuss this with your doctor or nurse. You will find more information in Chapter 6: The intrauterine device (IUD).

When can I have the emergency IUD removed?
If you do not want to keep the emergency IUD as your regular method of contraception it can be removed during your next period. If it's removed at any other time you will need to use additional contraception, such as condoms, for seven days before the emergency IUD is taken out. This is because sperm can live inside your body for up to seven days and could fertilise an egg once the emergency IUD is removed.

Chapter 18: Using contraception after you've had a baby

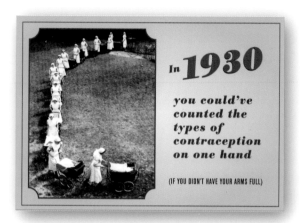

In **1930** you could've counted the types of contraception on one hand

(IF YOU DIDN'T HAVE YOUR ARMS FULL)

Contraception can be used throughout your lifetime, including just after you've given birth. Contraception may be the last thing on your mind when you are looking after a new baby but it's something to think about if you want to avoid or delay another pregnancy. Many unplanned pregnancies happen in the first few months after childbirth so it's better to be prepared by choosing your post-pregnancy contraceptive method before you have sex again.

How soon can I have sex again?
You can have sex as soon as you and your partner want to. Having a baby causes many physical and emotional changes for both partners and it may take some time before you feel comfortable or ready to have sex. Everyone is different, so do not feel pressured or worry that you are not normal if you don't feel ready to have sex. It can help to talk to a partner about any concerns you have.

When will my periods start again?
The earliest your periods can return is six weeks after birth if you are *not* breastfeeding. If you are breastfeeding your periods will return and you will start ovulating when you are breastfeeding less often and for shorter periods of time. You can become pregnant before your periods return because ovulation occurs about two weeks before you get your period.

How soon do I need to use contraception?
You need to start using contraception from three weeks (21 days) after the birth. Don't wait for your periods to return or until you have your postnatal check before you use contraception as you could get pregnant again before then. If you are

fully breastfeeding you can choose to rely on this for contraception. (See *Will breastfeeding act as a contraceptive?* below).

When can I start to use contraception?

- You don't need to use any contraception in the first three weeks after the birth as it is not possible to become pregnant in this time.
- You can use male and female condoms as soon as you want to.
- You can start to use the contraceptive implant from three weeks after the birth.
- If you are **not** breastfeeding then you can use the combined pill, the contraceptive vaginal ring and the contraceptive patch from three weeks after the birth.
- You can start the progestogen-only pill any time after the birth.
- It is usually recommended that you wait until six weeks after the birth to start the contraceptive injection because then you are less likely to have heavy and irregular bleeding. It is possible to use it earlier if there are no alternatives you find acceptable.
- An IUD or IUS is usually fitted from four weeks after a vaginal or caesarean birth. It can also be put in within 48 hours of the birth.
- You can start to use a diaphragm or cap six weeks after giving birth.
- Natural family planning can be used at any time.

Which contraceptive method will be suitable for me?

This depends on what you and your partner prefer, your medical history, any problems you had in your pregnancy and if you are breastfeeding. You can read more about each method including emergency contraception in Chapters 3–17 and ask your doctor, nurse or midwife for more advice.

Will breastfeeding act as a contraceptive?

Breastfeeding is also known as lactation. When used as a contraceptive method it is known as lactational amenorrhoea (LAM). LAM can be up to 98 per cent effective in preventing pregnancy if all of the following apply:

- you are fully breastfeeding – this means you are not giving your baby any other liquid or solid food **or**
- you are nearly fully breastfeeding – this means mainly breastfeeding your baby and infrequently giving your baby other liquids **and**
- your baby is less than six months old **and**
- you have no periods.

The risk of pregnancy increases if:
- you start breastfeeding less often, or
- there are long intervals between feeds – both day and night, or
- you stop night feeds and use supplement feeding.

Once your baby is over six months old the risk of getting pregnant increases, so even if you don't have periods and are fully or nearly fully breastfeeding, you should use another contraceptive method.

Will contraception affect the breast milk?
- If you are using a hormonal method of contraception a small amount of hormone will enter the milk, but no research has shown that this will harm your baby.
- It is usually advised that you wait until the baby is six months old before you start using the combined pill, the contraceptive vaginal ring or the contraceptive patch. This is because these methods contain the hormone estrogen which can reduce your milk flow.
- Using the IUD does not affect your milk, and copper from it does not get into the milk.

Will I need a rubella (German measles) vaccination?
During your antenatal care you will have had a blood test to see if you have had rubella. If the test showed you were not immune during your pregnancy you will probably be offered a rubella vaccination soon after the birth. It is very important **not** to get pregnant for one month after a rubella vaccination as it can harm the baby.

Do not have this vaccination if:
- you are, or think you may be, pregnant **or**
- you have recently had sex and could be pregnant.

Where can I get advice?
You can find out more about contraception from your midwife, nurse or doctor in hospital or from your midwife or health visitor at home. You and your partner can also visit your general practice, or a contraception or sexual health clinic. You can also contact FPA for information about contraception.

Chapter 19: Safer sex

While your contraception is protecting you against an unplanned pregnancy is it protecting you from sexually transmitted infections too?

If you are having sex you need to think about whether you could catch or pass on a sexually transmitted infection – an infection that can be passed to another person through unprotected vaginal, anal or oral sex. Some sexually transmitted infections can be passed by genital contact alone (between the penis, vulva, vagina or anus) or through sharing sex toys.

This chapter explains how safer sex can help you to avoid sexually transmitted infections, gives you tips about using condoms and dams – including how to talk to a partner about using them – and provides useful information about getting sexual health tests and check-ups.

Sexually transmitted infections

Some of the most common sexually transmitted infections are:
- chlamydia
- genital warts (human papillomavirus or HPV)
- genital herpes
- gonorrhoea (clap, drip, sting)
- non-specific urethritis (NSU).

Less common sexually transmitted infections are:
- trichomonas vaginalis (TV)
- pubic lice (crabs)
- scabies (itch)
- hepatitis B
- syphilis (pox)
- HIV.

Can they be treated?

Most sexually transmitted infections can be treated and it is usually best if treatment is started as soon as possible. Some infections, such as HIV, genital warts and genital herpes never leave the body but there are drugs available that can reduce the symptoms. Drugs can also help prevent or delay the development of complications in HIV. If left untreated, many sexually transmitted infections can be painful or uncomfortable and can permanently damage your health and fertility, and can be passed on to someone else.

How will I know if I have an infection?
Not everyone who has a sexually transmitted infection has signs and/or symptoms. Sometimes these don't appear for weeks or months and sometimes they go away, but you can still have the infection and pass it on to someone else. If you experience any of the following you should seek advice:
- unusual or smelly discharge from the vagina
- discharge from the penis
- pain or burning when you pass urine
- itches, rashes, lumps, ulcers, sores or blisters around the genitals or anus
- pain and/or bleeding during sex
- bleeding between periods
- bleeding after sex
- pain in the testicles
- pain in the lower abdomen (area above the pubic hair).

Even if you don't have any signs and/or symptoms you may wish to seek advice or have a check-up, particularly if:
- you have had unprotected sex with a new partner recently
- you or a partner have sex with other people without using a condom
- a sexual partner has any symptoms
- you are planning a pregnancy and may have been at risk of infection.

Where can I go if I am worried I might have an infection?
You can get all tests and treatments at a genitourinary medicine (GUM) or sexual health clinic. General practices, contraception clinics, young people's services and some pharmacies may also provide testing for some infections. If they can't provide what you need, they will be able to give you details of the nearest service that can.

All advice, information and tests are free, but if you go to a general practice you may have to pay a prescription charge for any treatment.

What will happen when I visit a sexual health clinic?
When you go for a sexually transmitted infection test you will not automatically

be tested for all infections. All tests are optional and should only be done with your permission. Sometimes you will get the results straightaway and sometimes you will have to wait. The service will explain how you get the results.

Tests for both men and women may include:
- An examination of your genitals, mouth, anus and skin to look for obvious signs of infection.
- Testing a sample of your urine.
- Having blood taken.
- Taking swabs from the urethra and any sores or blisters.
- Taking swabs from the throat and the rectum. This is less common.

In women the tests might also include:
- Taking swabs from the vagina and cervix.
- Having an internal examination.

Wherever you go for a test, you shouldn't be judged because of your sexual behaviour and all services should be confidential. Make sure you ask as many questions as you want to and get answers that you understand.

The staff at the service will offer you as much support as you need, particularly if you need help on how to tell a partner, and previous partners. This is strongly advised. The service may be able to offer you a 'contact slip' to give or send out to your partner(s) or, with your permission, the clinic can do this for you. The slip explains that they may have been exposed to a sexually transmitted infection and suggests that they go for a check-up. It may or may not say what that infection is. It will *not* have your name on it, so your confidentiality is protected. This is called partner notification.

In addition to tests and treatments for sexually transmitted infections there may be other services available at the sexual health clinic, such as:
- special sessions for people who have been sexually assaulted
- psychosexual counselling (to help with sexual problems)
- hepatitis B vaccination.

Safer sex

Safer sex is when people take precautions to help protect themselves against pregnancy and sexually transmitted infections.

Using contraception will help to protect you against an unplanned pregnancy but only condoms will help protect you from sexually transmitted infections too.

It's possible to get a sexually transmitted infection by having sex with someone who has a sexually transmitted infection but no symptoms, or to pass one on without knowing you have a sexually transmitted infection. Help protect yourself and others from most sexually transmitted infections by following these tips.

- Male and female condoms, when used correctly and consistently, are the best way to help protect yourself against sexually transmitted infections. Use condoms (male or female) every time you have vaginal or anal sex. If you can, avoid using spermicidally lubricated condoms. The spermicide commonly contains a chemical called Nonoxinol 9, which does not protect against HIV and may even increase the risk of infection.
- If you have oral sex, cover the penis with a condom or the female genitals and male or female anus with a latex (rubber) or polyurethane (plastic) square. This is often known as a dam.
- Women who rub their vulva against a female partner's vulva should cover the genitals with a latex or polyurethane dam.
- Avoid sharing sex toys as these can transfer sexually transmitted infections from one person to another. If you do share them, wash them or cover them with a new condom before anyone else uses them.

Tips for using condoms and dams

A lot of people are aware that condoms and dams will protect them from sexually transmitted infections but despite their best intentions, don't use them during sex. There are many reasons for this. For example, someone may:
- not know when to use them
- not know where to get them
- not know how to use them properly

- find it difficult to talk to a partner about using them
- not have found a condom that is comfortable
- get too wasted on drink and drugs to worry about using one.

This section will help to answer all of your questions and worries about condoms and dams. You can also find more information about using male and female condoms in Chapters 13 and 14.

When should I use condoms as contraception?

You can either use male or female condoms on their own as your method of contraception, or you can use a different method to help protect against an unplanned pregnancy and condoms to help protect against sexually transmitted infections. Protecting yourself against unplanned pregnancy *and* sexually transmitted infections will leave you free to enjoy sex just that bit more.

Where can I get male and female condoms?

Find out more in Chapter 13: Male condoms and Chapter 14: Female condoms.

Dams are available *free* at some sexual health services and can be bought at pharmacies and by mail order or online. If you do not have a dam available, make one by carefully cutting up a male condom.

- First unroll the condom and cut off the tip.
- Then cut down one long side and open it into a square. This can be used as a dam.
- If you are using a lubricated condom you may want to wash the lubricant off first if this tastes unpleasant. If you can, avoid using spermicidally lubricated condoms, see page 111 for more information. You may prefer to use a flavoured condom.
- You could also cut up a female polyurethane condom to make a dam. This is particularly useful if you or a partner are sensitive to latex.

Look after your condoms and dams
Find out more about how to look after condoms in Chapters 13 and 14.

Store dams in a cool, dry place, keeping them away from direct sunlight. Heat and moisture will damage them so that they are more likely to have holes.

Using condoms correctly

It is very easy to use male and female condoms but if you are not sure how to use them read our step-by-step guides in Chapters 13 and 14.

Using dams correctly

- Before you use the dam, check to make sure there are no holes or tears in it. Dams are often packaged with a powder on their surface and you may want to rinse this off under running water before you use one.
- Hold the dam against the vulva or anus. It will not stay in place unless somebody holds it. You can then have oral sex in the same way you would if the dam wasn't there.
- For extra sensitivity, apply a lubricant to a partner's vulva or anus before using the dam. Make sure you use the right sort of lubricant – see page 155.
- Only use one side of the dam – don't flip it over – and do not re-use a dam. If you have sex again, use a new dam.

Using lubricant

Using lubricant is a personal choice but it can increase your sexual pleasure by heightening sensation and making sex more comfortable. It also makes sex safer because it reduces friction and the risk of damage to the penis, vagina, vulva or anus, therefore reducing the risk of an infection being passed on. Always use lubricant for anal sex as the anus has no natural lubricant.

You can use lubricant with condoms and dams. Try massaging lubricant into each other, or putting it on (not in) the condom, or under the dam. Use it during masturbation or sex, lubricating the fingers, penis or sex toy before penetration. You can also buy lubricants that tingle, warm up and are flavoured. Don't use too much though – extra lubrication can make a condom slip off and can lessen the sensation for women.

If the condom or dam is made from **polyurethane** you can use any type of lubricant. However, it the condom or dam is made from **latex** you should never use oil-based products – such as body oils, creams, lotions or petroleum jelly – as a lubricant because they can damage latex.

Beat bedroom embarrassment – how to talk about condoms and dams

Do you find it difficult to talk about using condoms or dams with a partner? Some people say it makes them feel uncomfortable, unprepared, insensitive, judged, judgmental, worried, nervous, unloving, unsexy, and a whole host of other emotions! But it doesn't have to be like that.

Start the conversation

- It doesn't matter how old, young or sexually experienced you are, whether you are male or female, talking about (and using) condoms or dams can be a challenge for *everyone*. If you find it difficult to talk to a partner about condoms or dams, they might find it just as difficult to talk to you. Make the first move.
- It may help to rehearse what you want to say in advance, whether that be weeks before you have sex, or in the bathroom just beforehand! Think about the points you want to get across.
- Time your chat well – don't talk naked! If you can, talk to a partner away from the bedroom, without pressure and before you have sex.

- If you are worried that talking about condoms or dams in advance will make it seem like you are expecting sex, talk about that too!

Overcome your embarrassment

- Admit to being embarrassed. A partner might feel as embarrassed as you do.
- You won't be as embarrassed if you are confident using condoms or dams. Practice putting them on, taking them off, unwrapping and touching them. You could try putting one on a vegetable (for example, a carrot or courgette) or on a sex toy. If a partner says that they don't know how to use a condom, show them how and encourage them to practice too. Similarly, buy or make a dam. Put one on your skin (for example, on your arm) and explore the taste and feel of it.
- If you are embarrassed to buy condoms, get them from a sexual health service. No one there will be embarrassed. Or you could buy them online or ask a partner to buy them.
- If you are anxious that someone will see you carrying condoms or dams, take them out of the packet and put them in a tin or wallet, or wrap the packet in something else.

Talk about what you both want, and why

- Using condoms or dams means you are looking after *your* own sexual health – not making judgments about anyone else's sexual history. Try not to be concerned that a partner will question your motives if you want to use a condom or dam. If they do, explain to them that you are looking after *yourself* and that wanting to use a condom or dam has nothing to do with your view of them.
- If a partner suggests using a condom or dam don't be offended, and don't presume it's because they've got a sexually transmitted infection.
- If you suggest a partner uses a condom or dam and they tell you that they haven't got a sexually transmitted infection and don't need/want to use one, don't give in and have unprotected sex. You have a lot of options – ask them what bothers them, try gentle persuasion, tell you can make it fun, suggest you wait or don't have sex.

Encourage your partner

- People use all sorts of excuses for not using condoms or dams so be ready with your answer. For example, if a partner says that condoms are expensive, suggest you get them free at a contraception, sexual health or GUM clinic. Or if a partner says they don't have a dam, suggest you make one from a condom.
- 'But you're/I'm on the pill' is not a reason to stop using condoms. It's true that the pill will prevent pregnancy but condoms are the only way to help protect yourself from a sexually transmitted infection.
- If you or a partner are sensitive to latex you can use male or female polyurethane condoms or a polyurethane dam instead.
- If you or a partner thinks that condoms don't fit properly, experiment with different sizes and shapes.

- People sometimes worry that using condoms or dams takes the pleasure away from sex. They can be made sexier – and won't interrupt spontaneity – if you use them as part of sex, for example, during masturbation, or try using a dam with lubricant.
- Some men are concerned that using a condom will cause them to have erection or ejaculation difficulties. Using lubricant or condoms designed to heighten stimulation or delay ejaculation can all help.
- Alcohol and drugs might make you less likely to use condoms or a dam so make sure you get condoms and dams in advance. If you plan ahead, the more likely it is that you'll use condoms and dams.

Useful organisations

- FPA
- Brook
- Health and Social Care in Northern Ireland
- Health of Wales Information Service
- National Chlamydia Screening Programme
- NHS Direct
- NHS Scotland
- Terrence Higgins Trust

Contact details are listed in Chapter 22: Useful organisations.

Chapter 20: What if...?

While using contraception – especially using the method that is right for you and your partner – reduces your risk of getting pregnant or a sexually transmitted infection, there are many reasons why you could find yourself worrying you might be pregnant or have an infection. Maybe the condom split or came off. Perhaps you got carried away and didn't use a condom or maybe you forgot to put on a new contraceptive patch. Whatever the reason, there is information and advice to help you follow the best course of action and make the decision that is right for you if things don't go according to plan.

What if I've had sex without using contraception?

If you have had sex without using contraception, or think that your contraception might have failed you, there are two emergency methods you can use:

- The emergency hormonal pill – must be taken up to three days (72 hours) after sex. It is more effective the earlier it is taken after sex.
- An emergency IUD – must be fitted up to five days after sex, or up to five days after the earliest time you could have ovulated.

For more information on using emergency contraception see Chapter 17: Emergency contraception.

What if I think I may have caught a sexually transmitted infection?

If you are worried you might have a sexually transmitted infection it is a good idea to have a sexual health check-up. For more information about sexual health services and sexually transmitted infection testing see Chapter 19: Safer sex.

What if I think I might be pregnant?

If you (or a partner) could be pregnant do a pregnancy test as soon as possible. The earliest and most reliable sign of pregnancy for women with a regular menstrual cycle is a missed – or shorter and lighter – period. You can do a pregnancy test from the first day of a missed period. If you do a test before this time the level of pregnancy hormone, human chorionic gonadotrophin (hCG), may be too low to show up on the test and you may get a negative result even though you are pregnant. If you don't know when your next period is due, the earliest time to do a test is three weeks (21 days) after unprotected sex.

You can buy a pregnancy test from a pharmacy to do yourself, or you can ask for a test to be done at:

- your general practice
- a contraception clinic
- a young people's service (there will be an upper age limit)
- a pharmacy (there may be a charge)
- most NHS walk-in centres (England only)
- some sexual health or genitourinary medicine (GUM) clinics.

If the pregnancy test is positive this means you are pregnant. All tests, including tests you do yourself, are very reliable if you test at the right time. This may bring out a range of feelings in you – happiness, shock, worry, anxiety, excitement, concern or fear. All of these are normal.

However you feel, it's important to take the time to make the decision that's right for you but it's also important not to delay in making your decision. Don't let anyone else pressure you into doing something that you don't want to do. The decision is yours. For some women it can be very difficult working out what to do, but there is help and support available to help you think through your options.

Help and support

Talk to people you trust and get accurate information and advice about all your options. You may want to talk to:

- The FPA helpline
- The FPA unplanned pregnancy service in Northern Ireland
- your partner, family or friends
- a doctor or nurse at your general practice
- staff at a contraception or sexual health clinic
- staff at a young people's service (these will have an upper age limit)
- staff at a fee-paying organisation.

Contact details for these organisations can be found in Chapter 22: Useful organisations. It is essential that you are given accurate information and time to explore how you feel so that you can make the decision that is right for you. Be aware that some organisations may not offer unbiased pregnancy counselling or advice and may lead women into making the wrong choice for them.

If you are facing an unplanned pregnancy, you have three options. You can choose to:

- Continue with the pregnancy and keep the baby.
- End the pregnancy by having an abortion.
- Continue with the pregnancy and have the baby adopted.

Continuing with the pregnancy

If you decide to continue with the pregnancy you need to start your antenatal care (care during pregnancy), whether you are planning to keep the baby or to have it adopted. To start your antenatal care you can visit your general practice, or register with one. Or you may be able to go directly to a midwife at your nearest maternity unit. To find your nearest maternity unit go to Birth Choice UK or call NHS Direct (see Chapter 22: Useful organisations).

As part of your antenatal care, the doctor or midwife can talk to you about:

- healthy eating and exercise
- taking folic acid
- stopping smoking
- cutting out, or down on, alcohol
- stopping recreational drug use
- whether any medicines you are taking are unsafe during pregnancy
- getting advice and tests for sexually transmitted infections.

If you have a medical condition, such as epilepsy or diabetes, talk to your doctor or midwife as soon as possible because you may need special care. If you are taking medication, it is important that you continue to take this and seek advice from a doctor or nurse as soon as possible.

Help and support

There are many organisations that can offer help and information during and after your pregnancy. You can find contact details for these in Chapter 22: Useful organisations.

- Frank
- National Childbirth Trust (NCT)
- NHS Choices
- NHS Pregnancy
- NHS Smokefree
- Royal College of Obstetricians and Gynaecologists
- Tommy's
- Working Families.

For more information you can read the FPA booklet *Planning a pregnancy*.

Extra help after the birth

You may be worried that you won't be able to cope with looking after a baby. Knowing what help might be available may help you to make a decision about your pregnancy. You may be able to get help from:

- **Your partner, family and friends**. Think about who might be able to help you once the baby is born. If people you trust can help with things such as doing the shopping or looking after the baby, it can be a great support, and enable you to have sometime to yourself.
- **Your midwife or health visitor** can offer advice and support, and put you in touch with local groups where you can meet other new parents or get the support you need.
- **Social services** at your local authority can assess whether you might need extra support. They may be able to provide services such as nursery or day care, or a support worker who can come to your home.
- **Home-Start**. A volunteer may be able to visit you at home to give free practical and emotional help. You can go directly to your local Home-Start or you can be referred by your doctor, practice nurse, midwife, health visitor or social services.
- **Sure Start** offers help in early education, childcare and family support. Sure Start operates differently in England, Scotland, Wales and Northern Ireland but you can contact them for further information.

Abortion

Abortion, up to the 24th week of pregnancy, is a safe and legal way of ending a pregnancy in the UK, regardless of your age. However, getting an abortion can vary throughout the UK, and it can be very difficult to obtain an abortion in Northern Ireland. Abortion after 24 weeks is legal in certain circumstances (for example, if it is less likely to cause harm to a woman's physical or mental health than continuing with the pregnancy, or there is a substantial risk of physical or mental disability if the baby was born). This is not common.

It is important not to delay making your decision. Legal abortion is safer and easier the earlier it is done in pregnancy. It is important to get advice as soon as possible because it can take up to a month before the abortion is carried out. The abortion may be done sooner if you pay for it. There is no difference in the quality of care you should receive if you choose to pay for an abortion privately or go through the NHS.

Where to go if you want an abortion

Abortion care is available free through the NHS, or through other clinics and hospitals for a fee (the cost will vary).

- You can go to your general practice, local contraception or sexual health clinic or young people's service. They can refer you for an abortion through the NHS.
- It can be very difficult to get referred for an abortion in Northern Ireland. Women in Northern Ireland can contact the FPA unplanned pregnancy service. Advisers will be able to tell you about getting a private abortion in England if that's what you decide to do.
- You can directly contact organisations that provide abortion for a fee – you do not have to be referred by another service. Contact details for organisations like these can be found in Chapter 22: Useful organisations.

Confidentiality

Any woman who has an abortion, whatever age she is, has a right for that information to remain confidential. This means that the information cannot be shared with anyone else without your agreement. If you have any worries about confidentiality discuss this with the doctor or nurse you speak to about your abortion.

- Your GP does not need to know, although many abortion services like to send a letter to them. This should only be done with your permission.

- Your partner, or the father of the child, does not have to know about the abortion, and he has no legal rights to make a decision about whether or not you continue with the pregnancy. You can go ahead with an abortion without your partner's knowledge or agreement.

All information, advice and services are confidential but healthcare professionals are obliged, with your knowledge, to involve social services if they suspect you, or another person, to be at significant risk of harm (for example, sexual or physical abuse).

Help and support

For some women, deciding whether they want to have an abortion is easier if they know how an abortion is carried out. There are different abortion procedures and the method used depends on how long you've been pregnant. You can find out more from:
- The FPA helpline
- The FPA unplanned pregnancy service in Northern Ireland
- bpas
- Marie Stopes
- NHS Choices
- The Royal College of Obstetricians and Gynaecologists.

Adoption

Adoption could be a choice if you do not want to have an abortion but do not want to bring the baby up yourself. Adoption is a way of giving the baby new parents who will have legal rights and responsibilities for the child once the adoption is complete. It is a formal process organised by adoption agencies and local authorities and made legal by the courts. Once an adoption is made legal the decision is final and cannot be changed.

The adoption process

Although you can start preparing for adoption at any time during your pregnancy, the adoption won't be completed until after the baby is born. You will be asked to sign a formal document agreeing to the adoption, but you cannot be asked to do this until the baby is six weeks old. This agreement does not make the adoption final.

Usually, the baby will go to foster carers for a short time while arrangements are made for him or her to move to the adoptive parents. The adoptive parents will then look after the baby, and apply to the court for an adoption order. Once the order is granted, the adoption is final and you will no longer be the baby's legal parent.

You can change your mind at any stage before the adoption has been made legal but it may not be easy or even possible, to get your baby back, depending on how far the adoption has progressed. The court will make a decision based on what is best for the baby. Once the adoption has been made legal, the baby will stay with the adoptive parents even if you change your mind.

If you are considering adoption, the social worker or adoption agency that is supporting you will arrange special adoption counselling. This is to make sure that you know exactly what adoption involves, and to explore all the possible options so that you can make the right decision for you.

Help and support

Making the decision to have a baby adopted can be very difficult. If you think you might want to continue with the pregnancy and have the baby adopted you may find it helpful to talk to someone who can tell you more about adoption. You could talk to:
- the doctor or nurse at your general practice
- a social worker at your hospital (contact the hospital to find out if there is a social worker attached to the maternity unit)
- an adoption social worker at your local authority's social services department or at a local voluntary adoption agency
- the British Association of Adoption and Fostering (see Chapter 22: Useful organisations).

Contraception after pregnancy

It may be difficult to think about contraception soon after you've had a baby or an abortion but many unplanned pregnancies happen in the first few months so it is better to be prepared.

You will need to start using contraception immediately after an abortion or three weeks after having a baby. Don't wait for your periods to return as it is possible to get pregnant before then (ovulation happens around two weeks before a period). All methods of contraception can be used straight after an abortion.

For more information see Chapters 3–17 about contraceptive methods and Chapter 18: Using contraception after you've had a baby .

Useful organisations

- **FPA**
- **Abortion Rights**
- **Birth Choice UK**
- **bpas**
- **British Association for Adoption and Fostering**
- **Brook**
- **Calthorpe Clinic**
- **Frank**
- **Home-Start**
- **Marie Stopes**
- **National Childbirth Trust**
- **NHS Smokefree**
- **Royal College of Obstetricians and Gynaecologists**
- **Social services**
- **South Manchester Private Clinic**
- **Sure Start**
- **Tommy's**
- **Working Families**

Contact details are listed in Chapter 22: Useful organisations.

Chapter 21: Useful resources

FPA resources

Information booklets

Using expert medical advice and consumer research, FPA has developed a range of booklets about sexual health, individual methods of contraception, sexually transmitted infections, pregnancy choices, abortion and planning a pregnancy. They answer commonly asked questions and are updated regularly. Find out more at **www.fpa.org.uk** or call the FPA helpline.

Other resources

There are many other resources about contraception, having a baby, abortion, adoption and sexual health that you may find helpful. If the book contains medical information it is important that you read the most current edition as content and advice will change over time.

Barlow D, *Sexually Transmitted Infections: the Facts* (Oxford University Press, 2006).

Gebbie A and White K, *Fast Facts: Contraception* (Health Press, 2009).

Guillebaud J and MacGregor A, *The Pill and Other Forms of Hormonal Contraception (the Facts)* (Oxford University Press, 2009).

Lord J, *Adopting a Child: A Guide for People Interested in Adoption* (British Association for Adoption and Fostering, 2008).

National Childbirth Trust, *Get Closer – Humps and Bumps* (National Childbirth Trust, 2006).

Payton J, *Abortion – The Essential Guide* (Need2Know, 2009).

Royal College of Obstetricians and Gynaecologists, *Sterilisation for Women and Men: What You Need to Know* (Royal College of Obstetricians and Gynaecologists, 2004).

Smith N, *Understanding Pregnancy* (Family Doctor Publications, 2006).

Szarewski A and Guillebaud J, *Contraception: A User's Handbook* (Oxford University Press, 2000).

Chapter 22: Useful organisations

This chapter provides contact details for the organisations that offer further information and advice on the topics discussed in this book.

How FPA can help you

sexual health direct is a nationwide service run by FPA. It provides:

- confidential information and advice and a wide range of booklets on individual methods of contraception, common sexually transmitted infections, pregnancy choices, abortion and planning a pregnancy
- details of contraception, sexual health and genitourinary medicine (GUM) clinics and sexual assault referral centres.

FPA helplines
England
helpline 0845 122 8690
9am to 6pm Monday to Friday
Northern Ireland
helpline 0845 122 8687
9am to 5pm Monday to Thursday
9am to 4.30pm Friday
or visit the FPA website **www.fpa.org.uk**

Unplanned pregnancy in Northern Ireland
If you are faced with an unplanned pregnancy and you live in Northern Ireland, FPA in Northern Ireland can offer:

- non-judgemental and non-directive counselling
- information on all your options to help you decide what to do.

FPA in Northern Ireland also offers a counselling service for women who have had an abortion.

For an appointment, call FPA in Northern Ireland on 0845 122 8687. The service is confidential.

Getting help locally

You can get sexual health help and advice (including free contraception) in your area from:

- a general practice (unless they say they don't provide contraception services)
- a contraception clinic
- a sexual health clinic
- a young people's service (these will have an upper age limit)
- some GUM clinics.

You can also get free emergency contraception from:

- most NHS walk-in centres (England only) and minor injuries units
- some hospital accident and emergency departments (phone first to check)
- some pharmacies (there may be an age limit).

Other organisations

Abortion Rights

www.abortionrights.org.uk

The national pro-choice campaign site provides information about what to do if you are pregnant and considering abortion.

Birth Choice UK

www.birthchoiceuk.org

Helps women to choose where they want to give birth.

bpas

Tel: 08457 30 40 30

www.bpas.org

Information and advice on pregnancy and pregnancy choices, including abortion.

British Association of Adoption and Fostering

Tel: 020 7421 2600

www.baaf.org.uk

Advice and information about adoption and fostering in the UK.

Brook

Tel: 0808 802 1234

www.brook.org.uk

Clinics offering sexual health advice and contraception for young people up to 25.

Calthorpe Clinic

Tel: 0121 455 7585

www.calthorpe-clinic.co.uk

Provides abortion services for both private and NHS clients.

Fertility UK

www.fertilityuk.org

The national fertility awareness and natural family planning service.

Frank

Tel: 0800 77 66 00

www.talktofrank.com

Confidential drugs information and where to go for help.

Health and Social Care in Northern Ireland

www.n-i.nhs.uk

Health information for people in Northern Ireland.

Health of Wales Information Service

Tel: 0845 46 47

www.wales.nhs.uk

Health information for people in Wales.

Home-Start

Tel: 0800 068 63 68

www.home-start.org.uk

A charity helping families with young children.

Marie Stopes

Tel: 0845 300 8090

www.mariestopes.org.uk

Information and advice on sexual health, including contraception and abortion.

National Childbirth Trust (NCT)
Tel: 0300 33 00 772
www.nct.org.uk
Information on pre-pregnancy care and health of pregnant women, local antenatal classes, postnatal support groups and breastfeeding counsellors.

National Chlamydia Screening Programme
Tel: 0800 567 123
www.chlamydiascreening.nhs.uk
Information about chlamydia, accessing local services and how to get tested in the national screening programme.

National Osteoporosis Society
Tel: 0845 450 0230
www.nos.org.uk
Information and advice about osteoporosis.

NHS Choices
www.nhs.uk
Information on conditions, treatments, local services and healthy living.

NHS Direct
Tel: 0845 46 47
www.nhs.uk
Health information for people in England.

NHS Pregnancy – the pregnancy care planner
www.nhs.uk/pregnancy
An interactive pregnancy planner from NHS Choices for preconception onwards.

NHS Scotland
Tel: NHS 24 on 0845 4 24 24 24
www.show.scot.nhs.uk
Health information for people in Scotland.

NHS Smokefree

Tel: 0800 022 4332

www.gosmokefree.nhs.uk

Information about free NHS services to help people stop smoking.

Nuffield Health Hospitals

www.nuffieldhealth.com

Independent private hospitals that provide male and female sterilisation and male sterilisation reversal.

Relate

Tel: 0300 100 1234

www.relate.org.uk

Counselling, sex therapy and relationship education supporting couples and family relationships.

Relationships Scotland

Tel: 0845 119 2020

www.relationships-scotland.org.uk

Counselling, mediation and family support in Scotland.

Royal College of Anaesthetists

www.youranaesthetic.info

Information on anaesthetics for anyone having a local or general anaesthetic during surgery.

Royal College of Obstetricians and Gynaecologists

www.rcog.org.uk

Provides patient information on various topics, including abortion and health during pregnancy.

Sexwise

Tel: 0800 28 29 30

Information for young people on contraception.

Social services

You can find the number for social services in the local telephone directory for your area or on www.direct.gov.uk which lists all public services, including social services.

South Manchester Private Clinic
Tel: 0161 487 2660
www.smpclinic.co.uk
A private clinic providing pregnancy advice and abortion.

Sure Start
Tel: 0870 000 2288
www.surestart.gov.uk
Government programme bringing together early education, childcare and health to deliver support to young families.

Terrence Higgins Trust
Tel: 0845 1221 200
www.tht.org.uk
Information on safer sex, HIV and late stage HIV infection.

Tommy's
Tel: 0870 777 3060
www.tommys.org
Information and publications on pre-pregnancy health, pregnancy, miscarriage and stillbirth.

Vegan Society
Tel: 0121 523 1730
www.vegansociety.com
Information on ways of living free from animal products including vegan condoms.

Working Families
Tel: 0800 013 0313
www.workingfamilies.org.uk
Information and help for parents and families on all aspects of working and family life.

References

1. Office for National Statistics, *Contraception and Sexual Health 2007/08* (Office for National Statistics, 2008).

2. 958 women aged 18–49 years old in the UK were surveyed via the GfK NOP face-to-face omnibus survey. The survey was nationally representative. Weighting was applied to the data to bring it in line with national profiles. The research was conducted between 4–16 December, 2008 for the FPA Contraceptive Awareness Week (9–15 February, 2009).

3. FPA, *Revealed: Men's Attitudes to Contraception*, FPA Publishes Results of National Survey. FPA press release, 11 February 2008 (FPA, 2008).

Index